The Real Life Scenario Survival Handbook

Debbie Barham

SUMMERSDALE

Text by Debbie Barham

Summersdale Publishers Ltd
46 West Street
Chichester
West Sussex
PO19 1RP
UK

www.summersdale.com

Printed and bound in Great Britain.

ISBN 1 84024 283 3

CONTENTS

PREFACE: A Word from The Author 5

CHAPTER ONE: Medical Emergencies
How To Treat Broken Wind 7
How To Treat A Broken Heart 10
How To Deliver A Baby 15
How To Survive Sagging Breasts 19
How To Treat A Shopaholic 22
How To Keep A Big Brother Addict Alive Between Series 24
How To Cure A Mockney Accent 27
How To Survive A Massive Electric Charge 30
How To Survive A Near-Death Experience 32

CHAPTER TWO: Surviving Domestic Mishaps
How To Wrestle With An Obstinate Duvet Cover 33
How To Defrost A Freezer 40
How To Deal With A Red Wine Stain On Clothing 42
How To Construct An Item Of Self-Assembly Furniture 43

CHAPTER THREE: Survival On The Move
How To Pilot A Micro Scooter 45
How To Conceal An Unwanted Erection On Public Transport 50
How To Use An Aircraft Toilet 52
How To Survive Accidentally Ingesting A Railtrack Sandwich 59
How To Escape A Market Researcher In The Street 62
How To Break Into A Packet Of In-Flight Peanuts 65
How To Be Discreetly Sick In A Taxi 68
How To Obtain A Tolerable Passport Photo 71
How To Survive When Stranded In The Mountains With A Royal Skiing Party ...78
How To React When Your Offspring Is Kissed By An MP 82
How To Escape A Drunk And Disorderly Conviction 84
How To Survive A Celebrity Survivor Show 85
How To Wear A Skimpy Bikini On The Beach 92
How To Remove A Skimpy Bikini 95

CHAPTER FOUR: Survival In The Workplace

How To Survive A Random Outbreak Of Firing 99
How To Deal With A Stockmarket Crash Victim 102
How To Break Into The Modelling Industry 105
How To Rob A Bank 110
How To Escape From A Maximum Security Jail 113
How To Deal With A Charging Credit Card 117
How To Spot A Lying Politician 119
How To Climb A Greasy Pole 120
How To Disguise The Fact That You Are The Only Person In The Office Not
To Find Frasier Funny 122

CHAPTER FIVE: Surviving Sport and Leisure Activities

How To Save A Test Match 126
How To Avoid Being Stuck Behind A Big-Haired Person In The Cinema 131
How To Survive A Karaoke Christmas Party 136
How To Feign Interest In Modern Art 138
How To Survive A Barbecue 143

CHAPTER SIX: Negotiating Perilous Social Minefields

How To Camouflage Your Inability To Cook 148
How To Be Complimentary When Confronted With An Exceedingly Ugly Baby 152
How To Evade Vegetarian Food 155
How To Fend Off A Former Partner On Jerry Springer 158
How To Find The Loo In A Huge Modern Gastro-Dome 160
How To Survive If The Earth Fails To Move (For Women) 164

CHAPTER SEVEN: Dealing With Dangerous Animals

How To Extract Your Leg From A Randy Dog 167
How To Avoid A Bite From An Angry Hamster 170
How To Survive An Alien Abduction 174

PREFACE
A Word From The Author

The principle behind this Book is simple. Not being Dead is better than being Dead on almost every occasion.

You never know what Fate may have in store for you. There's simply no way of telling what's around the next corner. Except for buying yourself a periscope, or one of those fancy GPS navigation devices. Or asking somebody. But we British wouldn't dream of doing that even if it *was* a life-or-death situation.

Real Life is fraught with potential opportunities for loss of life, limbs, freedom, dignity, memory, credit cards, mobile phones, and stomach contents. The Author wants you to be prepared for every Real Life eventuality. To understand the importance of wearing the correct Survival Apparel, such as something other than an Arsenal shirt when in the immediate vicinity of Elland Road. To keep cool when threatened with the words 'Prepare to die!' by a merciless pension plan salesperson.

The Author is uniquely qualified to write a Book of this nature, on account of not yet having perished horribly in a freak using-the-wrong-fork-at-a-dinner-party incident, or gone Missing in Action after venturing into the labyrinthine voicemail system of Barclays telephone banking service.

Before writing this Book, the Author herself was not a professional Survivalist, but simply an ordinary everyday person like you with a morbid interest in potentially fatal accidents. She spent much of her childhood under canvas (on account of her parents being exceedingly rich and owning a large collection of valuable oil paintings), and has since slept under the stars on a number of occasions (the most memorable occasion being when she slept under a star from *Eastenders*, but she doesn't like to talk about that).

She now regularly guides teams of Young Conservatives, Advertising Account Directors and Fund Managers up the perilous slopes of Everest. And for the benefit of society at large, leaves them there to freeze to death.

So keep this Book handy at all times. It could save your life* and may also be employed to cover embarrassing genital arousal, squash an angry wasp, or deflect droplets of airborne spit from particularly ill-mannered blind dates. When spread with low-fat margarine, it will sustain the hungry explorer for several days and tastes infinitely better than a Blueberry Nutri-Grain bar.

Above all, do what the Boy Scouts do. Avoid being alone in a small tent with a bearded, middle-aged troop leader whom you're convinced you recognise from *Crimewatch Photocall*.

Because you just never know.

'Desperate' Debbie Barham
Royal London Hospital (Acute Spinal Injuries Ward)

*But most probably won't; a gun, a Sherpa tank or a satellite phone would be much more useful in almost every situation.

Disclaimer: the Author takes no responsibility for loss of life, money, credibility or much-loved pets arising from use of the techniques outlined in this Book.

CHAPTER ONE

Medical Emergencies

How To Treat Broken Wind

It must be something I ate....

Locate the most likely source of the Flatulence.
Pivot your gaze from side to side, then stand on the spot
and rotate your body to ensure you have fully assessed

your surroundings. In windy conditions, the Fart may drift several hundred metres from its original emission point.

If your own rectal passage is the source of the Fart, look around anyway and continue doing so for a protracted period of time.

This will help to conceal your guilt. Now locate the second most likely source of the Flatulence.

Ascertain whether women or children are within the danger zone.

If so, you may be able to blame the Fart on them. Women will be too embarrassed to deny it; children will merely be proud of their wind-breaking capacity.

Shoot the 'culprit' an accusatory gaze.

Aim carefully. If your boss is in the immediate vicinity, do not give them the impression that you think he or she is the Farter (even if this is the blatantly obvious truth).

If you are in an enclosed space, such as a train carriage or office lift, alert people to the danger.

Wrinkle your nose and oscillate your hand in front of your nose in a fanning motion. Only utter the words 'PooooEEEEE! Who trumped?' if you are under the age of six, or a medical student.

Do not call the police and request a sniffer dog.

However, if one arrives on the scene you may be able to blame the animal for the stink.

Breathe through your mouth, or through a handkerchief, until the hazardous gases have dispersed.

Do not crouch low on the ground where the air is clearer. This is EXTREMELY DANGEROUS as it will put your nose at buttock level and leave your nostrils vulnerable to subsequent attacks of Flatulence.

Vacate the scene of the Fart as quickly as possible.

When the doors of the lift or train carriage open, get out immediately, even if it isn't your floor or stop.

If you continue to experience Flatulence problems, consider changing your diet.

Do not scavenge for nuts, pulses and vegetables from the bean or legume family. These are high in protein and may exacerbate the problem. Instead, scavenge the shelves for unhealthy things like crisps and chocolate fudge cake.

Obtain a bottle of pine nut, walnut, or extra virgin olive oil.

A Mediterranean-style diet is believed to reduce Flatulent tendencies. More importantly, such oils are normally sold in corked bottles. Be alert for the early warning signs of Flatulence. When you get wind of an attack (or simply get wind), remove the cork from the bottle and insert it into the source of the potential Fart as a rudimentary bung or stopcock.

How To Treat A Broken Heart

Stem any external outpourings of grief by placing Kleenex over the eyes.
Immobilise the patient's arms and legs to prevent attempts at suicide or accidental bumping into hard, painful objects (e.g. their bastard/bitch of an Ex).

The patient may appear confused and disoriented.
It is quite natural for the patient to experience mild memory loss and failure to recognise their Ex as a right shitbag. The patient may also be under the impression that they have not, in fact, been dumped, but have actually carried out the dumping of their own volition.

If necessary, cut the patient free of their sexy apparel and/or Pulling Pants.
The patient is now single and can wear recuperative support garments, such as big, cosy jumpers and tracky bottoms.

Give the patient a shoulder to lean on whilst preventing him or her from wandering around and banging things.
The patient is in a vulnerable state and may bang someone really ugly in a drunken one-night stand which results in chronic embarrassment (or pregnancy).

Do not undertake to kiss it all better, no matter how much you fancy the patient.

The patient is in the Rebound Position. It is not advisable to remove the patient's clothing and feel his or her body all over for signs of horniness.

Apply emergency band aid.

Immerse the patient in bands such as The Carpenters, Wet Wet Wet and The Smiths. It may also be useful to administer 10cc.

The patient may be incapable of normal speech.

This should improve over time as the patient recovers the ability to say things other than 'I thought she loved me!', 'BASTARD!' or 'How COULD he – with my best friend?'

Insert a digit into the patient's mouth to check that the airway is not obstructed by the entire contents of a box of chocolate chip cookies.

Comfort-eating is a common symptom of Post-Relationship Trauma. The patient should not be left alone with unguarded high-calorie foodstuffs until heartbreak begins to heal.

Ensure the patient does not have access to dangerous objects, such as:

Knives
Firearms
Their Ex
A phone
Alanis Morrisette albums
Unattached members of the royal family.

If necessary, apply a tourniquet to the patient's forearms to prevent deliberate cutting of the wrists.

Or arms, or crotches of their Ex's designer clothes. This may result in an angry rash of legal action.

Assess whether the patient has been particularly badly hurt.

Have they, for instance, lost a significant amount of pride, jointly owned furniture, or Pink Floyd records?

Check that the patient has not suffered any serious loss of balance.

Has the break-up left a large hole in the patient's joint account? If so, it is important that you prevent the patient from deliberately O/D-ing (overdrafting).

Soothe wounded pride by liberal lubrication with flattering comments.

Concentrate these on the bum, breast and/or todger areas.

Excessive crying can lead to dehydration. Encourage the patient to drink a little fresh vodka or Jack Daniels.

In particularly tragic cases, it may be necessary to administer two or three pints of tequila slammers. Ensure that the patient is well plastered.

If the patient appears to have been hurt especially badly, a little pot may also be necessary.

Look for puffy joints (normally available from your local drug supplier). When the patient has smoked enough weed, he or she will no longer care about being given the old heave-ho.

Using a sharp scalpel, perform a Heartless Ex Bypass operation.

Carefully cut the Ex out of all photographic records of the recently severed relationship.

Explore the possibilities of fixing up the patient.

See if you have any single friends who can see the lovesick patient at short notice. If possible, book an appointment for a drink or trip to the cinema. The patient will probably need to see someone on a regular basis, two or three times a week. If you cannot find the patient a vacant bed immediately, get the patient onto the waiting list for a dating agency.

Pet Therapy is an alternative remedy recommended by many trauma counsellors. Interaction with domestic animals can greatly facilitate the healing process.

If the patient has recently split up with her boyfriend, she may miss having a companion in the house who scratches his bollocks and slobbers all over her friends. Getting a dog may fill this aching void.

Acupuncture may have beneficial effects for female (or homosexual) patients.

Point out that the patient's Ex only had a tiny prick anyway. Do not, however, insert a series of needles into the patient's skin. Getting a tattoo when under the influence of a broken heart is never advisable.

Seek expert guidance.

Consult your household copy of the latest Nick Hornby or Tony Parsons novel for the latest up-to-date advice on Broken Heart Aftercare.

How To Deliver A Baby

1. If You Are A Bloke

Prepare for the birth well in advance.

Make sure you are stocked up with vital equipment such as miniature Adidas Predator football boots, PlayStation games, copies of *Practical Parenting* magazine, Hornby train sets, Nick Hornby novels about Sensitive New Dads, and CDs of horrid whale music that sound like Bjork played backwards through a station Tannoy.

Rehearse the arrival of the Baby.

Do this by encouraging your partner to pour water all over the kitchen floor and shout hysterically at you, then panic because you can't find the car keys and phone your mum to ask what the hell you should do.

When the waters break, tell your partner to relax.

If this is a normal birth, she will respond by replying: 'RELAX? What do you mean, RELAX? I'm having a SODDING BABY!'

Pile the expectant mother into the car.

Drive to the nearest hospital. Try to resist the temptation to drive to the nearest petrol station for a bright yellow Baby on Board sign for the rear window.

Be prepared to deliver the Baby in adverse conditions where no proper equipment or medical assistance is available.
Such as an NHS maternity ward.

Keeping your voice as calm and soothing as possible, gently encourage your partner to push.
Emit an embarrassed laugh when your partner points out that the door of the delivery room actually says 'Pull' on it.

Enter the delivery room and wait for the contractions to increase in frequency. Hold your partner's hand.
Help her to relax by making inane comments and offering to get some sandwiches or something.

When the demands for you to push off come at 2–3 minute intervals, retreat to a safe distance. Pace around nervously.
Avoid dehydration by imbibing at least 28 cups of unidentifiable, tepid, greyish-coloured liquid from the hospital coffee machine.

Enter the delivery room just in time to see your partner re-enact what appears to be the scene in Alien *where a hideous, mucus-covered alien incubus bursts out of John Hurt's stomach. If everything is going according to plan, you will lose consciousness at this point and need to be revived by qualified medical professionals.*

Wait for the midwife to slap you sharply with the palm of her hand until you open your mouth and start screaming.

Locate the umbilical cord.

Deliver a trite remark about your offspring being exceedingly well endowed before the midwife cuts it off.

Enthusiastically offer to change your first nappy.

Use a bucket of detergent and a J-cloth to clear up the vomit (yours, not the Baby's).

Disappear down the pub.

Bore all your mates by incessantly talking about your child.

Repeat the step above for 18 years, or until your child leaves home.

2. If You Are A Woman

Prepare for the birth well in advance. Make sure you are stocked up with vital equipment such as clean towels, hot water and soap.

DO NOT leave this to your partner. He is a bloke and will rarely, if ever, have encountered clean towels, hot water or soap, and certainly won't have a clue what to do with them.

When the contractions begin, carry out the following procedure:

1. Get yourself to a hospital. (DO NOT attempt to deliver the Baby in the back of a taxi. The Baby will probably take twice as long to arrive, having 'taken a short cut', and its first words will be 'Blaaaadhy Tories, eh? And wot about all them illegal immigrants?')
2. Experience EXTREME and AGONISING pain.
3. Scream 'GIVE ME AN EPIDURAL NOW!!!'
4. Repeat steps 2 and 3 until fully anaesthetised.
5. Push.
6. Breathe.
7. Repeat steps 5 and 6 until Baby's head appears.
8. Feed Baby.
9. Burp Baby.
10. Repeat steps 8 and 9 for 18 years, until Baby goes off to university.

How To Survive Sagging Breasts

Try to ascertain the age of the Breasts.

Breasts corrode with age. Older mammaries are more susceptible to slipping down the chest and causing fatal injuries.

Look for any warning signs that the Breasts are about to sag.

These could include papery, wrinkled skin, a decrease in pertness, or a large red triangle bearing a picture of two tumbling boulder-like items and the words 'Beware: Falling Breasts'.

Determine the extent of the Breastdroop.

Do the Breasts hang lower than your hemline? Do your nipples concuss small children whom you pass in the street? Can you tie them in a knot, tie them in a bow or toss them over your shoulder like a regimental soldier? Are you frequently mistaken for Charlie Dimmock?

If you can tie them in a knot (or bow), do this at the earliest opportunity.

Unsecured Breasts are a hazard to short people, children and domestic animals. Utilise the granny knot if you are over the age of 60 or have particularly low-hanging Breasts. Otherwise, loop the Breasts across the chest and tie a loose sheepshank or double reef.

Do not, however, toss them over your shoulder like a regimental soldier. Even if you can.

This too can inflict severe bruising upon yourself and others.

If you cannot tie the Breasts in a suitable knot, fasten a red flag to each nipple.

This will serve as a warning to approaching pedestrians. Failure to indicate Hazardous Breasts is a crime under the Highways Act of 1952 (Section 5, subsection iii, Bumpers and Headlamps).

Try to locate a vein.

If you are able to locate lots of prominent blue veins protruding from the Breasts, slippage is imminent.

Take immediate action. Shore up the Breasts with a large safety net, such as that used by Tightrope Walkers.

If there is no Big Top within a 5-mile radius, improvise by securing the Breasts with any convenient item (e.g., garden hammock, deep-sea trawler's net, Marks and Spencer's Underwired Multiway Support Bra).

Drive to a plastic surgery clinic immediately.

Do not worry about exceeding the speed limit. In the event of a crash, your Breasts will act as both driver-side and passenger-side airbags.

Instruct the plastic surgeon to make a swift incision above each Breast and haul them upward by a distance of at least six inches.

He may use industrial lifting gear or a block-and-tackle if necessary.

Repeat the operation every time the Breasts begin to slip.

Only cease the process when the skin has been so frequently lifted that your nipples have toenails.

How To Treat A Shopaholic

Do not treat the Shopaholic to a day out at the Lakeside Retail Complex.

Retail therapy is not a proven method of conquering shopping addiction.

Try to rehabilitate the Shopaholic into the wider community.

Encourage the Shopaholic to mix with crowds of people in the street, though preferably not Oxford Street whilst waiting for the Selfridges sale to begin.

Take the Shopaholic down the pub, or to an environment where hard drugs are readily available.

Becoming an alcoholic or smackhead will take the Shopaholic's mind off his or her latest must-have item.

Consult a recognised support organisation, such as Shopaholics Anonymous.

Encourage the Shopaholic to attend regular meetings, at which fellow sufferers can sit around in a circle with bags over their heads (to stop themselves from filling the bags with unwanted impulse-buys).

Try over-the-counter remedies, such as the Harvey Nicorette Patch, which can be applied to the reverse of a credit card to prevent excessive department store purchases from being made.

Caution! Obtaining such over-the-counter remedies over the counter may, in some cases, exacerbate the condition.

Take the recovering Shopaholic routinely for check-ups.

Do not take the recovering Shopaholic routinely to checkouts.

How To Keep A *Big Brother* Addict Alive Between Series

Try to prevent the addiction before the onset of total Big Brother *dependency.*

Stay alert. Do you notice changes in the person's behaviour: has he or she developed a glassy-eyed expression and sluggish reactions? Is he or she suddenly refusing invitations to social events? Does he or she no longer respond to your telephone calls (due to being permanently engaged on the *Big Brother* eviction hotline?) Does he or she refer to 'housemates' and imagine they are his or her friends, even though he or she lives entirely alone? Is he or she paranoid that the housemates' every move is NOT being watched by hidden cameras? All may indicate early symptoms of chronic *Big Brother* addiction!

When the victim's regular Big Brother *fix is withdrawn, try to ensure that someone is with the victim to prevent him or her from doing anything stupid.*

This may not be physically possible if the victim is too heavily under the influence of Jade Goody or Helen Adams.

Assess the severity of the addiction.

Is the victim in a Persistent Vegetative State, induced by having been sat in the same armchair staring at the TV for three months without a break? The victim should slowly recover the power of normal speech. Stay by his or her side and talk to the victim. Do not expect a response. When the victim regains brain functions, he or she will probably have no recollection of anything that's happened in the outside world during the past twelve weeks. This is perfectly normal for a reality TV addict.

Gently wean the* Big Brother *addict onto intelligent broadcasting by introducing less habit-forming reality TV programmes, like* Airport, Bargain Hunt *or* Pop Idol.

Do not expose the addict immediately to well-made dramas, thought-provoking documentaries or BBC2 discussion shows. Such unaccustomed pressure on the brain will probably cause massive cranial haemorrhage and instant death.

If the victim still appears not to have a life without* Big Brother, *more drastic measures may be required.

Get the victim to a WHSmith's and purchase the *Big Brother* book, novelty pop records by ex-*Big Brother* contestants (MC Amma, Jade Goody as J-Go, 'Somethin' Stupid' by Paul and Helen) and the Big Brother boxed DVD set.

Ensure that the addict receives proper nutrition during the period between series.

Many *Big Brother* addicts simply waste away and die, incapable of obtaining small regular intakes of food and drink unless prompted to do so by the words 'Back after the break'.

If the victim shows no signs of returning to normal social functions, take steps to ensure that the victim is admitted to a residential institution for those with similar mental subnormality, where his or her behaviour can be properly monitored and where watching Big Brother *is physically impossible.*

In other words, persuade him or her to apply as a contestant for the next series.

How To Cure A Mockney Accent

Stay alert. Listen carefully to the speech patterns of those around you.
Remember the maxim: 'Accents may happen, even in the best regulated families.'

Do you mix with television presenters, aspiring stand-up comedians, pop stars, Brit Art enfants terribles, radical film directors or trendy young novelists?
You are in a high-risk group. It is exceedingly likely that a Mockney Accent may be transmitted. Probably on Radio One.

Adopt a seated posture in front of the television set and familiarise yourself with the remote control.
Place *Mary Poppins* in the VCR and press the Play button, normally indicated by a small green arrow.

Carefully observe and memorise the mannerisms of Dick Van Dyke.
Try to avoid fits of laughter, which may disturb passers-by and lead them to believe that you are suffering an epileptic fit.

Should you notice similar sounds emitting from the mouths of your friends, alert them to the situation.

They may not be aware that they are starting to talk like a wanker.

Look through the victim's address book under their surname.

This will indicate the location of the victim's parents. Point out to the victim that his dad lives in Amersham, he is a nice well-brought up Home Counties boy, and he probably went to a very expensive public school. He is not a fick kid from an Ackney estate wiv nah dosh anna bruvva ooza bittuva geezah.

If normal speech is not resumed, you may need to use force.

Caution! Bad Mockney accents can be highly contagious. Wrap a scarf or similar item around your ears to prevent accidentally picking up Estuary English mannerisms. Place a rolled-up handkerchief in your mouth to prevent the dropping of any loose H's.

Approach the Mockney Speaker from behind and deliver a sharp blow between the shoulder blades.

Continue doing so until a coughing sound is produced, indicating that the vowels stuck in the victim's throat have been expelled.

When the victim regains the power of normal speech, ask if he knows his name and birthplace.
If he still claims to be a cheeky chirpy Cockney sparrer, guv, lawksamussy apples-and-pears, repeat the above process.

If the Mockney Accent fails to subside, more drastic measures must be employed to prevent the affliction infecting the wider community.
Get yourself to a dodgy East End boozer as quickly as possible and hire a chirpy Cockney contract killer. Ensure that the victim is bumped off immediately.

Under NO circumstances should you hold a traditional East End gangland funeral, remarking on how the Deceased was a diamond geezah oo might've been a bad lot but 'e luvved 'is old mum.

How To Survive A Massive Electric Charge

Brace yourself for a huge shock from the electricity.
This normally comes once every quarter in the form of a small brown envelope through your letterbox.

Use a sharp knife or razor blade to make an incision in the envelope. Remove the contents and unfold.
Your body may begin to shake involuntarily and your limbs may jerk around in the air. Do not touch anyone else until this behaviour has subsided and your body has gone limp.

Ask a trusted friend or colleague to break it gently to you what the damage is.
You may well have lost an arm and a leg.

Check your wrist for a pulse: you may have suffered a heart attack as a result of the trauma.
In the event of a heart attack, lick your fingers and ram them into an electric socket. The voltage should be sufficient to revive you.

Once the damage has been assessed, immediately switch off all your lights and electrical appliances.
This may fool the debt-collectors into thinking you have gone away on holiday.

Keep warm by making a fire using suitable flammable materials as kindling.

Suitable flammable materials include: Electricity Bills, Electricity Bills (Final Demand), Electricity Bills (Absolutely Final Demand), Electricity Bills ('We Really Mean It This Time' Demand), Electricity Bills ('Look, Just Pay Up - We're Not Pissing About' Demand), Electricity Bills ('We've Sent The Boys Round To Break Your Legs' Demand), Court Summonses, and Collection Notices from Local Bailiffs.

Ensure that you are wearing several items made of vulcanised rubber.

Now that your electricity has been cut off, these will keep you much better insulated from the cold than garments made of cotton or nylon.

Be prepared to suffer repeated seizures in the future.

Bailiffs may seize your telly, your video and sometimes your microwave as well. None of which you will miss, since you no longer have any electricity left to run them on.

DO NOT attempt to commit suicide by sticking your head in the gas oven.

It is unlikely that you will have paid your gas bill either, so this will be entirely futile and a complete waste of time.

How To Survive
A Near-Death Experience

Just DO it.

That's why it's called a 'Near-Death Experience'. If you didn't survive, it'd be a 'Death Experience', wouldn't it? Duh.

CHAPTER TWO

Surviving Domestic Mishaps

How To Wrestle With An Obstinate Duvet Cover

Should it take two days to change a duvet cover?

Only tackle the Duvet Cover unaided if no external assistance is available.

Ring your mother, current or ex-partner, or local Social Services department, giving a brief and succinct description of your problem. They should immediately recognise the severity of the situation and come to your assistance.

If no assistance is forthcoming, assess the need for changing the Duvet Cover.
Is it:

a) Above 20 degrees in temperature?

b) Less than eight months (or five shags) since the bedclothes were last changed?

c) Impractical to just go out and buy a new one, demanding that you have the one in the shop window display with the cover already fitted?

d) King Size, e.g., approximating in size to the dimensions of the average football pitch?

e) A hotel room/student bedsit/someone else's bedroom that you're standing in?

If you can answer yes to any of the above, the Duvet does not require changing.

Close your eyes and stand ten paces away from the Duvet. Keep your mouth shut and inhale deeply through your nose.
Can you still smell the Duvet? If not, the Duvet does not require changing.

If changing the Duvet is unavoidable, first equip yourself with suitable tools.
You will need:

1) One (1) pot of lubricant (e.g., Vaseline, engine oil, KY Jelly)

2) One (1) grappling hook (large) and four (4) tent pegs

3) One (1) clean or comparatively clean Duvet Cover

4) One (1) scuba-diving helmet (inc. breathing tube)
5) One (1) powerful torch or flashlight
6) One (1) GPS positioning device
7) One (1) compass
8) Two (2) bars of Kendall Mint Cake
9) One hundred metres (100m) of strong rope or twine
10) One (1) Thermos of hot soup or liquid beverage
11) One (1) two-man ridge tent
12) Lots (lots) of tent pegs
13) One (1) clothes peg (optional)
DO NOT attempt to change the Duvet without first arming yourself with all of the above apparatus.

Stand well back from the Duvet. Ensure that the Duvet is not moving up and down in a gently undulating motion.

A moving Duvet may indicate the presence of a live organism beneath it. You should not attempt to change the Duvet without first ensuring that the bed is unoccupied. A sleeping partner may become violent and enraged if you remove the Duvet without prior warning.

Identify the clean Duvet Cover and place it on one side.

Form a large aperture in one side of the Duvet Cover by disengaging the poppers or buttons.

Emit a loud roaring sound from the back of your throat.

This may assist in scaring the Duvet into submission.

Perform a flying leap onto the Duvet Cover, spread-eagling your arms and legs as though making a parachute jump.

When you land, grasp a corner of the Duvet Cover with each hand and use your feet to immobilise the other two corners.

Without letting go of the outer cover, jerk your hands repeatedly in an upward direction to release the Duvet from the Duvet Cover.

Do not succumb to the urge to hold your nose, however overpowering the odour of the unclean Duvet Cover. You will need both hands free to wrestle the Duvet. If you have a low smell tolerance, place a clothes peg over the nostrils prior to attempting the cover change.

Form the unclean Duvet Cover into a ball shape and hurl it as far away from you as possible.

Aim it towards a laundry basket, washing machine, or open window. Do not aim it towards people or animals.

The Duvet should now be lying motionless in front of you.

Do not be fooled by its submissive posture. It is a dangerous beast and should only be tackled with extreme care, especially if it has a high Tog Rating.

Don your scuba helmet and place the breathing tube between the lips. Draw several breaths to ensure that the tube is not blocked and that you can inhale and exhale without undue discomfort.

You may wish to consume one bar of Kendall Mint Cake at this point, to replenish the glucose reserves needed to accomplish successful changing of the Duvet.

Tuck the torch, GPS device and grappling hook into your belt or waistband. Unfold the clean Duvet Cover and lay it flat in front of you with the aperture facing south.

Secure each corner of the Duvet Cover with a tent peg, ensuring that the aperture remains large enough to permit the entry of a human being.

Take a swig from your Thermos to prevent dehydration.

Try not to spill any of the contents on the clean Duvet Cover. You will not enjoy having to sleep on the wet patch.

Lie face down on the ground, and wriggle on your stomach towards the Duvet Cover.

Manoeuvre your body through the aperture until you are completely enveloped by fabric. Smear yourself with the Vaseline or other lubricant embrocation, if necessary.

Perform a 180-degree turn, so that your head is facing the aperture.

Extend your arms out of the open mouth of the Duvet Cover, and draw your two-man ridge tent inside. Erect your tent inside the clean Duvet Cover so that it supports the fabric and permits increased manoeuvrability within the enclosed space.

Consume your other bar of Kendall Mint Cake in preparation for the final battle. Exit the tent and grasp the Duvet, which should still be lying in a prone position.

If the Duvet attempts to rear up and attack you, subdue it with the grappling hook and roll it into a sausage formation, similar in size and shape to a human corpse.

Drag the rolled up Duvet through the aperture of the Duvet Cover, slinging it over your shoulder as though you were carrying an injured companion.

If you can, wrap the strong rope or twine around the rolled-up Duvet and secure with a series of nautical knots. Otherwise the Duvet may become enraged and unroll itself, attempting to smother you.

When the Duvet is fully inside the clean Duvet Cover, de-rig the ridge tent and ensure that no tent poles remain inside the Cover.

Leaving tent poles inside your Duvet Cover may inflict subsequent injury on yourself or your partner (if applicable) during sexual activity.

Release the Duvet from its bindings and allow it to unroll, retreating swiftly backward to prevent yourself from being asphyxiated.

Make your escape through the aperture, then seal the exit using the poppers or buttons to prevent the Duvet from pursuing you.

When you are sure the Duvet is calm and unprovoked, remove the tent pegs from each corner.

Draw the Duvet across the bed, ensuring all icky stains on the sheets are properly covered.

If you fail at any stage in the procedure, return to stage one of the procedure and restart.

Continue attempting to change the Duvet until nightfall. When it becomes too dark to change the Duvet, wrap yourself in several layers of warm clothing and sleep in the tent. Consume all remaining provisions to keep your strength up. Smear your entire body in lubricant to insulate yourself. Then consume the remaining lubricant, which will be high in fatty oils and therefore provide vital energy.

Repeat once per year.

Or move back in with your mother.

How To Defrost A Freezer

Ascertain that the freezer is due for defrosting.
You may notice any or all of the following:
1) Door incapable of being shut without aid of Sellotape.
2) Harpoon required to penetrate ice when attempting to snare packet of fish fingers.
3) Icy overhang or plateau extending several feet across kitchen.
4) Residency of Eskimo community in frozen pea compartment.
5) Request from Sir Ranulph Fiennes for permission to explore your Zanussi appliances.

Obtain a large ice axe and suitable apparel.
Your clothing should be sufficient to both insulate against the cold and repel tides of cascading water.

Important! Locate the instruction manual that came with your freezer.
This will burn well, and hasten the defrosting process.

Open the freezer door and begin chipping methodically at the ice.
Be on guard. Avalanches may occur at any moment without warning. An avalanche of ice can be exceedingly dangerous. However, an avalanche of frozen Weight Watchers Ready Meals, Lean Cuisines and 5kg bags of frozen Brussels sprouts which have been in there since 1994 can be fatal.

If you hear a creaking, cracking sound, run from the kitchen and close the door.

Do not return until you are sure the avalanche has subsided. This will be signified by a puddle of defrosted water gushing under the kitchen door.

Use your survival instincts to remain alive for the two or three weeks it will take a 24-Hour Plumber to come and rescue your kitchen.

Scavenge for fresh food in your local Sainsbury's. You will have to exist on nuts and berries for the foreseeable future, since your freezer is still defrosting and your kitchen is too badly flooded to venture into.

When rescued by a local Tradesperson, restock your freezer with emergency provisions.

Use powerful magnets to attach a large Hazard sign to the freezer door, warning you in future to defrost your freezer on a more regular basis, you bone idle so-and-so.

How To Deal With A Red Wine Stain On Clothing

Dab ineffectually at the stain with a napkin or tissue.

This will ensure that the stain is spread liberally around your clothing, rather than simply confined to one small area.

Apply plenty of cream to the affected area.

If you have no cream, rub in a generous quantity of cheese fondue or hollandaise sauce.

When you return home, place the clothing in your wardrobe.

Do not wash the clothing. Leave the cream to develop into a crusty white residue.

After four years or so, remove the clothing from the wardrobe.

Contact a tabloid newspaper and claim you were wearing it whilst indulging in oral sex with a noted celebrity (e.g., President of the United States, famous floppy-haired film actor, host of popular satirical panel game show on BBC2).

Bank the cheque you received for your story from the tabloid newspaper.

When the cheque clears, use the money to have the item of clothing professionally dry-cleaned.

How To Construct An Item Of Self-Assembly Furniture

Using a scalpel or Swiss Army Knife, release the Self-Assembly Furniture from its cellophane packaging.

Ask around to discover whether anyone in the locality has experience in building bivouacs or lean-to shelters using just a clump of palm fronds or some dried mud. Don't worry if they haven't. Such feats will seem like a piece of piss compared to constructing an Ikea coffee table.

Lay out the unassembled parts on a flat surface.
Ascertain that they look nothing like the diagram on the Assembly Instructions.

Manoeuvre the parts around in a half-hearted fashion for two or three minutes, vaguely poking them with a small screwdriver, and entirely failing to construct an item of trendy Scandinavian-style interior furnishing.
Remind yourself that a continuing inability to get it up is perfectly normal and in no way reflects badly upon your masculinity. If still worried, consider telephoning the Customer Support Line and asking for advice on Screwing and Erection Problems.

Carefully put the parts back inside the packaging.
Return immediately to the store. Demand a full refund on the grounds that their Self-Assembly Furniture is being sold on false pretences, because it quite patently doesn't assemble itself at all. Pursue the matter in court if necessary. Use your £1m compensation money to purchase a ready-built Philippe Starck coffee table.

CHAPTER THREE

Survival On The Move

> ## How To Pilot A
> ## Micro Scooter

Do not attempt to pilot a Micro Scooter if you are over the age of seven, except under extreme circumstances.

Extreme circumstances could include someone under the age of seven accusing you of being a boring old fart; you are totally pissed; you are a student.

Push, pull, carry or drag the owner of the Scooter away from the controls.

This should be easily facilitated, on account of the owner being under the age of seven and less than four feet tall.

Take up the Scooter-driving position.

Stand parallel to the Scooter with your feet placed slightly apart and your head facing forward.

If radio equipment is available, place the earphones over your head.

This will prevent you from hearing communication messages relayed by your seven-year-old audience, along the lines of 'Mind you don't fall off, Grandad!' and 'Cor, I bet Michael Schumacher is REALLY SCARED!'

Tune the radio to the emergency frequency for Kiss FM.

Do not tune the radio to Radio Two, Melody Radio or Radio Four, since this will merely reinforce the impression that you are a doddery old git.

Identify the controls, the braking pedal and the speedometer.

There should not be any. It's a sodding Scooter. It HAS no controls. If you can see a yoke, throttle, joystick, altimeter or instrument panel indicating airspeed and fuel consumption, STOP NOW. You are obviously trying to demonstrate your youthfulness by playing Microsoft Flight Simulator.

Do not say 'Mayday, Mayday!'

Because people will just laugh at you.

Mount the Scooter.

Bend down so that your nose drops to a height of not more than four feet. Grasp the handlebars with both hands. Place your right foot on the metal footplate, and push gently with the ball of your left (NB: the ball of your left foot. Not your left ball. This could result in serious physical injury).

You may begin to wobble.

Especially if you are, indeed, totally hammered.

Accelerate to a gentle cruising velocity.

Deploy the nonchalant comment about riding a Micro Scooter being a right piece of piss.

Increase your speed to a Standard Showing-Off Velocity of 70mph.

Inform pedestrians that you are approaching by shouting 'WHEEE! BEEP-BEEP!' or executing a poor impersonation of Murray Walker doing the commentary for the Hungarian Grand Prix.

Line up the front wheel, so that the kerb is just to the left of the nearside handlebar-tip.
Using your really expensive shoes, steer and brake the Scooter as necessary. Try to ignore the fact that your really expensive shoes will become scuffed, soaked, mudspattered and covered in dog shit. This is an Emergency.

Execute the necessary manoeuvres to accomplish your not looking like an old fart any more.
Performing a wheelie, bunnyhop or dazzling heel-brake turn will increase threefold your chances of impressing a seven-year-old. A poorly-executed manoeuvre in dangerous terrain (such as the shop floor of Tesco's, where security guards may give chase) is infinitely more impressive than a well-executed manoeuvre in your own back garden.

Listen out for detailed instructions.
Such as: 'I'm bored now! Oi! Can I 'ave me Scooter back, Gramps?'

Avoid that tree.
What tree?

That tree. THERE!
Ouch.

If you are lucky, you will land on soft ground or a grassy area.
By bending your legs on impact, the full force of the shock will be absorbed somewhat, allowing you to escape with just broken legs, arms and spectacles.

Lie still and do not attempt to get up.
This will fool your seven-year-old tormentors into thinking you are dead, and may prevent them from going away and returning with reinforcements to take the piss out of your misfortune.

How To Conceal An Unwanted Erection On Public Transport

Gently prod the swollen area.
Ensure that the bulge in your trousers is not due to a mobile phone or portable GPS device.

Assume a foetal position (see Fig 1a) with your hands clasped over your groin.
Cover your vulnerable crotch region with a strategically placed newspaper or copy of Jung Chang's *Wild Swans*.

Identify the source of the inopportune erection.
This may well be a scantily-clad female in the nearby vicinity.

If possible, cover her extremities with a warm garment.
Do not think about her firm, inviting breasts, smooth nubile thighs or silky underwear. This may cause a further rush of blood to the crotch, impairing your ability to escape and drawing unwanted attention to yourself.

Slowly and carefully start to contemplate Vanessa Feltz.
You should now feel the erection start to subside. Thinking about mortgage repayments, your spouse's mother or Robin Cook in a state of arousal may also prove effective.

If the swelling persists, evasive action is required.
Do not attempt to rub it better. Avoid making sudden, jerky motions which may attract charges of public indecency.

Do not loosen clothing around the affected area.
Unzipping your trousers will alarm fellow travellers. If you are travelling on a train approaching a tunnel, do not think about trains entering tunnels.

When the vehicle's motion begins to slow, assume a crouching posture beside the door.
As soon as the vehicle comes to a halt, leap to safety and hobble to a place of concealment such as a public toilet or telephone kiosk. It is normal to experience difficulty when running.

Dampen your ardour by applying cold water to the affected area as soon as you can.
Administering a large quantity of alcohol may also have a beneficial effect (this method is often referred to as Brewer's Droop).

In the event of the swelling failing to go down, seek help from a large photograph of Ann Widdecombe.

How To Use An Aircraft Toilet

1) For Urination Purposes

Take stock of your situation.
You are locked in a small airless box with no ventilation or means of escape.

Begin by removing the garments from the lower part of your body.
Try to gain access to your own genitalia. If movement is severely restricted, use the Complimentary Airline Liquid Soap as a rudimentary form of lubrication.

Take a deep breath.
Lift the lid, ensuring your nasal passages are blocked to prevent accidental inhalation of someone else's massive jobbie. Remember, previous passengers may have been subject to a vicious attack of diarrhoea perpetrated by biologically hazardous in-flight bolognese.

Brace your back against the door of the cubicle.
The door may be cunningly booby-locked to display the 'Vacant' sign whilst occupied, thereby lulling you into a false sense of security.

Locate the handbasin.
In most passenger aircraft, this is the small concave protrusion on the wall which looks like a soapdish and contains several hundred yards of wet lavatory paper and 300 cigarette butts.

Keeping your body rigid, manoeuvre your bottom into the handbasin.

DO NOT press the red button marked Hot Tap, or you may suffer 70 per cent burns on your left buttock.

Keeping both feet braced against the wall, aim your urine into the toilet bowl.

It helps to have suitable apparatus, such as a penis. If no penis is to hand, improvise using a rolled up copy of the in-flight magazine.

Allow your bladder to depressurise. When you are sure the pee has subsided, return your undergarments to the upright position.

Your feet may feel as though they are bound together with tight ropes. This is probably your trousers.

Tread water, and try to paddle towards the exit.

The water level around the toilet floor may have risen to a depth of several metres. Remove your shoes and socks, and inflate your rubber life jacket as demonstrated by the cabin crew. Do not blow your Emergency Whistle, since this may elicit a desire to start peeing again.

Wrest the door open by pulling with both hands.

The weight of water against the door may make this operation difficult to achieve. Once you have made your escape, navigate back to the Economy Class section of the plane. If the Stewardess attempts to offer you more drinks, hide under the seat and take evasive action.

2) For Sexual Purposes

Take stock of your situation.

You are locked in a small airless box with someone you know only tenuously. Try not to appear nervous. If you are a first-time in-flight shagger, it may help to imbibe a copious quantity of duty-free alcohol which will act as a muscle relaxant. If you are a man, do not imbibe TOO much duty-free alcohol or your muscle will be so relaxed as to make in-flight sex impossible.

Begin by removing the garments from the lower part of your partner's body.

Try to gain access to your partner's genitalia. If movement is severely restricted, use the Complimentary Airline Liquid Soap as a rudimentary form of lubrication.

Refer to your complimentary In-Flight Shagging Card, if one is available.

Adopt the Doggy Position, as shown. Grasp the seat in front of you firmly with both hands. Tug your partner's fly to inflate the genitals. Take a deep breath, place your lips over the mouthpiece and suck hard.

Open your partner's wallet and locate the protective rubber equipment.

Put on the protective equipment as directed by the very camp airline cabin steward.

Keeping your body rigid, manoeuvre your bottom into the handbasin.
DO NOT press the red button marked Hot Tap, or both you and your partner may suffer 70 per cent burns.

Try to recall the dirty bits from the in-flight film.
If the In Flight Film was *Home Alone*, Disney's *Fantasia* or *Mrs Doubtfire*, you may skip this stage.

Brace your back against the door of the cubicle.
Guide your partner through the shagging procedure, using your hands to manoeuvre the control stick from left to right. Remember that this equipment is highly sensitive and will respond to the slightest touch. If you have prior experience of airline sex, use suitable jargon like 'Roger, Roger' or 'Legover and out'.

Allow the genitalia to depressurise. When you are sure all desire has subsided, return the undergarments to an upright position.
Return to your respective seats. If the No Smoking sign is not illuminated, light up a post-coital cigarette.

3) For Solo Sexual Purposes

Take stock of your situation.
You are locked in a small airless box with no titillation or means of arousal, save for a well-thumbed copy of the in-flight magazine, the most stimulating aspects of which comprise a full page picture of a Rolex Oyster, a guide to packing the perfect suitcase and a feature on how not to catch dysentery when backpacking in Goa.

Abandon the procedure.
Have a dump or a fag instead (see Subsections 4 and 5).

4) For Defecation Purposes

Adopt the Crap Position, as shown on the in-flight safety card.
Sit well back on the seat with your legs closed, your bowels open and your head bent forward. Grasp firmly onto the nose in front of you.

Prepare yourself for a loud, explosive noise and the sound of high-pressure air rushing rapidly out of a small aperture.
You may also hear a splash as your turd hits the water.

Hold your breath and leave the cubicle as fast as possible. Do not stop to press the flush.
Employ the oxygen mask, until fresh air is available.

If challenged by fellow passengers, deny all knowledge of the massive keech in the khazi and claim you were merely in there having a quick J Arthur.

5) For Smoking Purposes

Close the door. Open the fag packet.
Remove the cigarettes from the packet. Ensure the cigarettes are not the Extra Long variety, which are unlikely to fit lengthways in the enclosed space of an aircraft toilet.

Place the previous sneaky in-flight smoker's cigarette butt in the toilet bowl.
Place your own butt on the toilet seat.

Smoke a cigarette.
Put your hands over your ears to protect yourself from guilty feelings about the queue of five desperate Germans banging on the door and shouting 'Mein Gott! Bist Du STILL in die Toilette?!'

If disturbed by an angry Stewardess, brandish your lighter.
Threaten to blow up the aircraft by lifting the toilet seat and igniting a pocket of fart-gas.

Continue smoking until the aircraft lands, then get yourself immediately to a duty-free retail outlet.
Purchase as many cigarettes as you can physically carry.

Engineer a distraction to divert the attention of security staff. Duck down and run past the passenger checkpoint. DO NOT pass through the designated Security Gate!
You may inadvertently see an X-ray of your own nicotine-clogged lungs, the shock of which is liable to trigger a fatal heart attack.

How To Survive Accidentally Ingesting A Railtrack Sandwich

Stay alert. When travelling on a crowded train, scan the carriage for any suspicious packages.
Be especially wary of those with a strong odour, or the words 'Best Before Aug 1986' on the wrapper.

If you see something you think is a sandwich, treat it with caution.
Do not EAT it with caution, or even with the plastic fork provided. It may well be highly toxic, and will also cost an absolute bomb. As a rail passenger, you are at the mercy of Buffet Car prices.

Alert other passengers to the danger and pull the emergency handle.
Do not pull the corner of the transparent packaging of the sandwich, indicated with an arrow and the phrase 'Open Here'.

Assess the extent of the hazard.
Analyse the ingredients label for the words 'Egg Mayonnaise', denoting maximum toxicity.

In the event of accidental swallowing of any morsel of the sandwich, purge the contents of your stomach without delay.

If you suffer from travel sickness, you may be able to induce sufficient nausea simply by sitting down in one of the seats facing the opposite way to the direction of travel.

Alternatively, a finger rammed into the back of the throat and repeated firm squeezing of the lower abdomen will often trigger vomiting. On most crowded commuter trains you will experience both of these whether you wish to or not. The finger will probably belong to some sweaty stockbroker with a BO problem, in whose armpit your nose is forcibly buried. This too may help to induce the puking mechanism, and will at least take away some of the smell of the Egg Mayonnaise.

Ensure that you throw up into one of the bags provided for this purpose by the rail operators.

Bags for being sick in are located in the Bag Rack. They are easily identified by having a luggage tag on the side bearing the address of an American tourist.

Continue barfing until you have expunged every molecule of the sandwich from your stomach.

Be aware of the risks of subsequent dehydration. Drink at least two glasses of warm water with weak sugar solution dissolved in it. You can obtain these by visiting the Buffet Car, ordering a couple of bottles of low-alcohol Kaliber Lager and handing over a twenty-pound note.

Accept your 37 pence change.

Do not be tempted to purchase another sandwich, however hungry you are. In the event of extreme starvation, kill and eat a fellow passenger or gnaw your own arm off.

How To Escape A Market Researcher In The Street

Stay near populated, well-lit areas.
The more people there are in the locality, the less likely the Market Researcher is to pick on YOU.

Avoid resembling an Average Man or Woman in the Street.
This is what the Market Researcher is looking for. Take steps to be less average. DO NOT:
Be between 18 and 35 years old.
Earn between £25,000 and £35,000 per annum.
Drive a Renault Clio.
Be married with two children.
Wear a size 14 dress (unless you are a man, in which case this is sufficiently non-average) and be on a diet.
Vote New Labour and be unable to name more than two members of the current Cabinet.
Watch Coronation Street, EastEnders, and that thing with Carol Vorderman where she does up people's houses.
Drink Coke.
Snort coke.
Support Manchester United.

Learn to recognise a Market Researcher from 50 paces.
A Market Researcher usually has bright eyes, a clipboard

and a shiny coat (often cagoule-style). Market Researchers usually work in teams. They are pack animals, and generally carry at least one pack of some new type of skincare product.

If you spot a Market Researcher on your tail, try to throw them off the scent.

Put your head down and walk with a determined sense of purpose, as though on the way to a business meeting.

Do not accept any free samples or incentives.

You may subsequently feel indebted to the Market Researcher and be duty-bound to answer a lot of intrusive questions about your daily breakfast regime.

Be suspicious of any beverage you are offered.

These may be laced with something addictive, such as caffeine, or a ludicrous amount of pure sugar disguised as Healthy Californian-style Fruit Juice.

Avoid giving out any personal details that would allow you to be traced.

A particularly persistent Market Researcher may continue to target you for many years, relentlessly chasing you with Free Prize Draw Entries, samples of shampoo, or pursuing you for your opinion about a new brand of cat food.

Carry emergency Marketeer-deterrent equipment.

If approached by a Researcher, ensure that you make the first offensive move. Whip out your own clipboard and biro, and fire off a salvo of questions about whether he/she has suffered haemorrhoids within the last (a) Week (b) Month (c) Year.

If this fails to deter the Researcher, ask whether the Researcher would be prepared to participate in a clinical trial of a new deodorant product.
Take out a can of Mace or CS gas (available from selected hardware stores) and spray liberally in the face of the Researcher.

Before making good your escape, ask the Market Researcher whether he/she is suffering:
    Red, watery eyes.
    Extreme pain.
    Streaming discharge from the sinuses.
    Fear and disorientation.
    All of the above.
Compile your findings into a table of helpful statistics which can be subsequently submitted to the relevant polling organisation.

How To Break Into A Packet Of In-Flight Peanuts

Assess the situation in a rational manner.
Count the number of peanuts in the packet through the foil.

If the packet contains fewer than nine individual peanuts, DO NOT attempt to release them.
Obtaining the peanuts from the plastic packet will expend more calories than their consumption can provide, and leave you in a weakened state.

Before tackling the peanuts, ensure that no other form of nutrition is available.
Can you lick the condensation from the aircraft window, suck sweat from a fellow passenger's armpit, or consume the contents of a used sick-bag? Failing that, can you force yourself to eat what looks like two postage stamps full of dog poo, but is in fact Meat Ravioli, on the in-flight meal tray?

If the peanuts are the sole source of sustenance open to you, begin to examine the packet.
Do you see any visible means of entry to the peanut packet? No, obviously not.

Scan the cabin for a sharp object, such as a knife or nail-clippers.

Do any of your fellow passengers look like potential hijackers? Are they wearing false beards and carrying bags marked BOMB? Do they have suspiciously well clipped nails with smooth, buffed cuticles? If so, alert the cabin crew. The ensuing panic may allow you the vital seconds you need to purloin the suspected hijacker's nail-clippers.

Attack the peanut packet, making repeated stabbing motions with your sharp object.

Punch and kick the peanut packet, calling for assistance from fellow passengers. If this is unsuccessful, ask to borrow the hijacker's gun and endeavour to puncture the packet of peanuts with a bullet.

Try to bite the plastic packet with your teeth.

This is unlikely to puncture the packaging, but may taste better than the Meat Ravioli and keep your energy levels up.

Ask the Air Stewardess for a cup of coffee, demanding that it be 'not too hot'.

IMPORTANT! Cover your groin area with your flip-down tray or in-flight magazine! The Stewardess will attempt to torture you by pouring scalding liquid into your groin until you confess to having not eaten all your Meat Ravioli.

Try to salvage some of the coffee by catching it in the coffee cup.

Place the peanut packet in the coffee cup. The boiling liquid may be sufficient to melt the plastic packet and permit access to the peanuts.

If all else fails, tackle the Air Stewardess in a headlock.

Be prepared for retaliation: she may try to choke you with a small dry crispbread.

Claim you are a militant activist from the Peanut Liberation Front and demand that the pilot land at the nearest available airport.

Upon landing, run to the nearest airport branch of WHSmith's and purchase a pair of scissors to open the peanuts.

Consume the peanuts.

Beware! Many people suffer from Nut Allergies. Packets of peanuts May Contain Nuts. Please check with your doctor before attempting the above procedure.

How To Be Discreetly Sick In A Taxi

If you wish to be sick in a taxi, it is imperative that you first consume sufficient food and drink.
Twelve Vodka Redbulls, a packet of pork scratchings and a King Prawn Jalfrezi from a moderately disreputable Tandoori Emporium is usually adequate provision.

Familiarise yourself with your surroundings.
You may notice a sign reading 'Fine If You Are Sick In This Taxi'. Ensure that you interpret this correctly. The sign indicates that a penalty is payable for vomiting in transit, NOT that vomiting in transit is fine and acceptable behaviour.

Attempt to provoke the driver into a vicious, political rant.
This is easily facilitated by uttering certain key words, such as 'Mrs Thatcher', 'immigrants' or 'unlicensed minicab drivers'.

If he fails to rise to the challenge, adopt Plan B and ask whether he has had anyone famous in the back of his cab recently, like that George Best or that Chris Evans off the telly.
If your Cabbie fails to respond, he is probably deaf as a post and will therefore remain blissfully unaware of your hawking up 12 Vodka Redbulls and a dodgy curry in the back of his vehicle.

When the rant is in full flow, adopt the Puke Position.

Lean slightly forward with your legs apart, your mouth open and any long hair tucked safely behind your shoulders.

Modern taxis are fitted with a special receptacle for passenger vomit. This is located behind the driver's compartment and disguised as an extra seat.

Fold down the vomit receptacle to facilitate the collection of the vomit.

Ensure that the vomit receptacle does not already contain the vomit of the previous passenger.

If vomit is already present, your driver is probably telling the truth about having had that George Best, or that Chris Evans off the telly in the back of his cab recently.

Aiming your vomit directly ahead of you, eject the contents of your stomach via the oesophagus and larynx.

Try not to splatter the transparent screen between yourself and your driver. This may distract him from his rant and cause him to retaliate by sticking another few quid on the meter for dry-cleaning charges.

Conceal evidence of your Technicolour yawn by returning the vomit receptacle to an upright position.

The vomit should remain safely inside for subsequent passengers to discover.

Continue your journey as normal.
Caution! It is advisable to insert earplugs where available, otherwise the driver's bigoted political views may induce further involuntary vomiting.

How To Obtain A Tolerable Passport Photo

Ensure that you allow enough time to obtain your passport or ID photo before you actually need to use your Passport or ID.

Developing a normal photograph will require several days' processing time. Obtaining a bearable passport photograph will take marginally longer.

71

First, locate a Passport Photo Booth.

This will be labelled something like 'Krap-Snap Xpress', 'Gross-Pix-O-Matic' or 'Foto-U-Like-An-Escaped-Mental-Patient'. You can easily locate the nearest photo booth by following the unmistakable smell of stale vomit and/or urine.

Check that the booth is unoccupied.

There may already be a person inside having a photograph taken. However, there is far more chance of there being a person or persons inside having a snog/a spliff/a piss/a shag/a bout of nausea/a drug-induced fit or a wank.

When you are sure the booth is empty, draw back the curtains.

In front of you will be a small sign. This will probably read 'Out Of Order'. Do not be fooled by the absence of an Out Of Order sign: this merely means that the person or persons using the booth before you has utilised the Out of Order sign as a substitute for bog roll or Rizla.

Exit the booth and try to locate another one.

It may be necessary to travel several miles in order to locate a booth which is (a) unoccupied and (b) functional. In extreme circumstances, you may have to travel to another country to accomplish this. Ensure that you have your passport with you to prevent undue delay at Customs. To circumvent your lack of a passport photo, obtain a fake passport bearing a picture of Geri Halliwell cut out of *Heat* magazine, and a plastic Hallowe'en mask resembling a skeleton (available from all good joke and novelty shops).

When you locate a functional passport-photo booth, enter immediately. In front of you will be a small stool.
This was probably excreted by an incontinent tramp at some point over the past seven days. Try to ignore it.

Place your bottom on the little metal seat.
You will obviously need plenty of rest after the exertion of finding a working booth.

Adjust the seat to the correct height by rotating it in a clockwise or anticlockwise fashion.
Bear in mind that the previous user of the booth will either have been a seven-foot-tall member of the Harlem Globetrotters, or Jimmy Krankie. You will know that the seat is at the correct height when you can see your face in the glass window opposite.

Ensure that your hair is messy, your clothes crumpled, and that you are wearing a wild-eyed expression reminiscent of a long-term inmate of Rampton top-security hospital.
Choose the most unflattering colour of curtain to suit your particular complexion. Options normally include pale blue (to make you look pasty), brownish orange (to make you look sick) and plain white (to make you look like a convict).

Familiarise yourself with the controls of the booth.
Directly in front of you will be a vertical aperture just large enough to accept a pound coin. It is also just large enough

to accept a lump of semi-masticated Wrigley's Extra or a screwed up train ticket, as you will discover when you attempt to insert your pound coin.

Clear the blockage from the coin aperture to permit smooth passage of the coin.

Try to ignore the snotty-sounding disembodied voice that keeps demanding that you Insert Correct Payment And Adjust Seat So Your Head Is In The Red Circle.

Insert the correct payment for your photographs.

At least one of your coins will be rejected for no apparent reason. This is a standard function of all passport photo booths which took many years of engineering to perfect. Rejection of your money merely serves to reinforce the opinion that you are some sort of criminal, attempting to perpetrate large-scale financial fraud.

Prepare for the photographic process to begin.

You will know when the photograph is about to be taken, because this is the point at which a disgusting child will stick its head through the curtain and say something highly offensive to you, thus ensuring that you take a swipe at the little brat and your first picture depicts just half of your face, mouthing 'sod off'.

Once the process is underway, DO NOT attempt to escape from the booth.

If you run away now, your photos will be purloined by the disgusting child who will probably deface them and pin them up in a public toilet somewhere.

Brace yourself for exposure to blindingly bright light.

If you have previously been kidnapped by Iraqi militia and subjected to inhumane interrogation procedures, this is only slightly more uncomfortable. DO NOT shield your sensitive retinas with a hand or screw your eyes up tightly. Nor should you wear powerful UV-protection sunglasses, unless you want a set of passport photos that make you look like a reject from *Reservoir Dogs*.

Smile.

If the face in the mirror appears to be baring its gaping, yellowish jaws at you in the manner of a rabid crocodile, stop smiling. You have bad teeth. Adopt a tight-lipped smirk and seek immediate dental advice on exiting the booth.

Rotating your shoulders by 45 degrees will apparently result in a more flattering shot.

As will rotating your face by 180 degrees, but this is rarely acceptable as an official ID photograph.

Wait for four flashes in rapid succession.

If your passport booth is in a particularly insalubrious location, you may also judge the time elapsed by waiting for four flashers in rapid succession.

Get up from the seat.

This will cause the machine to take its final shot, thereby ensuring that 25 per cent of your three quid has been spent on taking a photo of your crotch. You may, however, recoup this cost by sending your picture to one of the less discerning pornographic magazine publishers.

Stand outside the booth and wait for your photographs to be delivered.

This will take at least fifteen minutes. Photo booth technology is a complex science and it requires considerable time to develop your skin-tone to the most unprepossessing shade of puce possible.

Your photographs will be ejected from a slot in the side of the machine.

Into a pile of steaming dog poo, unless you are alert enough to perform a flying leap and catch them in mid-air.

Scrutinise your photographs to ascertain whether they meet the correct passport requirements.

Your four photographs should comprise:

1) Motion shot of half your head disappearing out of view.

2) Both eyes closed.

3) Both eyes open. But mouth also open, in slack-jawed manner of the educationally subnormal. Optional gobbet of drool dangling from bottom lip.

4) Full frontal close-up crotch shot.

None of the above comply with correct passport requirements as laid out by HM Government Home Office.

Re-enter the passport booth with whatever heavy implement you can find (hammer, brick, sock full of 10p pieces, your own forehead).

Smash the glass. Do not hesitate to consider the consequences. This is an emergency.

HOW TO OBTAIN A TOLERABLE PASSPORT PHOTO

Get to a telephone and call the Passport Booth Service Centre complaining that their machine is Out of Order.
Then dial 999 and report an incident involving a suspected escaped loony vandalising a photo booth.

When released from custody, ask police to give you an extra copy of your mugshot.
Affix this to your passport, where indicated. It will be infinitely preferable to anything obtainable from a Snap-U-Krap booth.

How To Survive When Stranded In The Mountains With A Royal Skiing Party

Learn to recognise the danger signs that denote an approaching Royal Tour.

Do you hear a rumbling noise in the sky that appears to be getting nearer? Is it made by a large, expensive-looking private jet? Is an avalanche of matching Louis Vuitton hand luggage beginning to move slowly down the mountain toward the resort? Are you temporarily blinded by the glare of paparazzi flashbulbs?

Try not to panic. You may, however, experience an uncontrollable shaking and terrified desire to retreat into your chalet and hide.

This is a medically recognised condition, known as Klostersphobia. It can only be cured by intensive psychotherapy.

Run from the area before you are engulfed by a mountain of white powdery snow,.

Do not endeavour to get as high as possible. Unless you are Tara Palmer-Tompkinson, and are doing so by snorting the mountain of white powdery snow through a rolled-up fiver.

Leave the resort immediately.
If you remain at the scene, you may unwittingly find yourself shot at by tabloid paparazzi.

Get as far away from the piste as possible.
This will lessen the likelihood of your encountering stray Royals.

Using whatever items of cutlery you have managed to salvage from the resort, build yourself a rudimentary igloo, snow-hole or other manner of temporary shelter on the side of the mountain.
Such accommodation will be extremely uncomfortable, but still preferable to sharing a five-star hotel with Princess Michael of Kent or Sophie Wessex.

Wrap yourself in thick woollen clothing to minimise the risk of exposure.
Unless you are Tara Palmer Tompkinson, in which case wrap yourself in a mink-trimmed La Perla bra-and-panty set, a pair of Miu Miu kitten heels and lots of make-up, in order to maximise potential exposure.

Keep an eye out for roaming animals such as bears, foxes and wolves.
If you spot any, warn them that Prince Philip is in the locality and may well have his hunting rifle with him.

Snowbound mountain climates are also home to a legendary, shaggy, man-eating monster with huge teeth and claws, known as Bigfoot.

But if you're lucky, the Royal Party might not include Sarah Ferguson.

To keep yourself warm, light a fire using whatever materials you can scavenge under cover of darkness.

Such as Fergie's old fag lighter and a pile of discarded, flammable acrylic ski trousers which she brought with her but can no longer get her arse into on account of too many grappas and fondues.

If you see any passing aircraft, signal that you want to be picked up by waving your arms and shouting 'Help, help' to alert the pilot.

Unless you are Tara Palmer-Tompkinson, in which case signal that you want to be picked up by waving your mink-trimmed La Perla knickers and shouting 'Fancy a shag? I love a man in uniform!' to alert the pilot.

The human body is capable of resisting extreme cold for long periods. To conserve vital resources, lie still and avoid moving around any more than is absolutely necessary.

Imagine you are a member of the Royal Family. Such enforced bone-idleness in alpine conditions will then seem like perfectly normal behaviour.

As your physical strength decreases, be prepared for hallucinations to set in.

You may experience disturbing visions, such as Prince Charles trying to look cool on a snowboard.

Until the Royal Party is scared away by the paparazzi, you can do nothing but wait and try to avoid starving to death. If you are lucky, rescue may arrive in the shape of a corgi with a barrel of whisky tied around its neck.

This will be addressed to Prince Harry, but your need is greater even than his. Harpoon the corgi with a well-aimed cocktail stick, drink the whisky and spit-roast the dog over a cigarette. This should provide you with sufficient energy to survive until the Royals have left the area.

How To React When Your Offspring Is Kissed By An MP

Do not struggle or shout.
This may alarm a rabid politician and provoke him into slugging you (or your offspring) with a powerful left hook.

Try to distract the politician with a more tantalising photo opportunity.
Wave some potentially-Foot-and-Mouth-infected British Beef under his nose, or pretend to be an old lady with a dodgy hip who's been kept waiting six months for an operation. Canvassing MPs will inevitably target the most weak and vulnerable members of society.

If the politician refuses to unclamp his jaws from your child, hit him with a difficult question about European Policy.
This is normally sufficient to scare away an electioneering MP.

Should the politician still persist in worrying your child, make a growling noise like a Jaguar.
Going 'Brmmm-Brmmm, Brmmm-Brmmmm' will fool him into thinking somebody is trying to nick his expensive car, and give you the vital seconds you need to snatch back your child from his slavering jaws.

Attend to your child immediately.
Place your mouth over the kissed region and suck out as much of the venom as you can.

Rub the area with anti-Eurosceptic ointment.
Ensure that your child is fully immunised against TB (Tony Blair).

When bitten by a creepy crawly politician, it is also advisable for your child to receive several jabs.
Though preferably not from the politician's clenched fist.

Can you see a large red mark or an area of blue discoloration on your child's body?
This may be a Labour or Conservative Rosette. Remove it straight away to prevent any unwanted political tendencies from developing.

Consult a Spin-Doctor to determine whether the politician is a threat.
If your child has been kissed by a Liberal Democrat, there should be no lasting effect.

Keep your children safely indoors until the outbreak of Election Fever subsides.
If your child is over the age of 14, or the kiss continues for more than 30 seconds (with tongues), get your child to a lawyer as soon as possible.

How To Escape A Drunk And Disorderly Conviction

Do not duck down and hide behind a stationary vehicle.

Do not try to leap from a moving car, especially not if the moving car behind it has a blue flashing light and is indicating for you to pull over.

Do not proceed in a zigzag fashion as though attempting to dodge a sniper's bullets.

Do not attempt to revive yourself with brandy.

Do not attempt to wrestle Officers of Her Majesty's Constabulary.

If you are apprehended with a drink in your possession, **do not** try to swallow the evidence.

Do not try to expel toxins from your system by vomiting repeatedly into a convenient receptacle, such as a small bag. You are only supposed to blow into it.
Especially do not try to expel toxins from your system by vomiting repeatedly into a convenient receptacle, such as a policeman's helmet.

Do not attempt to engage in dialogue with your captor.

Particularly not in dialogue which involves words of more than one syllable. This will be a dead giveaway that you're pissed as a fart.

Do not attempt to fly.

Either with or without the use of a small aircraft.

Do not try to keep your spirits up by singing songs or telling jokes.

Especially not rude ones about policemen.

Do not make universally recognised hand signals.

Particularly not those utilising only two fingers.

Do not enter the nearest building and demand help.

Particularly not if the nearest building is a pub.

Ask a passer-by to dial 999 and ask for the Police.

If you also ask the passer-by to report an exceptionally grisly murder in the near vicinity, the police will hopefully bugger off and attend the scene before they have time to arrest you.

How To Survive A Celebrity *Survivor* Show

Calmly and rationally assess your predicament.
You are most likely to be somewhere in the Australian outback, surrounded by washed-up radio presenters and dangerous, publicity-hungry bimbos.

Scrutinise your landing site to ascertain that there are no bodies in the area.
You will probably find five or six Nobodies, e.g., Darren Day, Tony Blackburn, and some lanky posh girl with big teeth and a coke habit.

Accept that in such a hostile, captive situation you are highly likely to be shot.
Normally by an ITV camera crew.

Boost your morale by concentrating on the prospect of your future release.
Your new-found fame should enable you to release a novelty pop record, tie-in book or behind the scenes TV show when your ordeal is finally over.

Do not scream, shout, howl, holler or wail at the top of your voice to attract attention.
This escape tactic only works on other reality shows, such as *Pop Idol* or *Fame Academy*.

Trust nobody!
Remember – this is a Live TV or death situation!

In such dire circumstances, it is not unusual for celebrities to turn on each other.
Your fellow hostages may attempt to turn you on by flashing their breasts at you, 'accidentally' losing their underwear in the jungle, or trying to grope you under the pretext of killing a venomous snake in your crotch.

Prepare for the onset of inclement weather by building a rudimentary A-frame shelter.
Bind together two stiff wooden objects at an angle of 35 degrees. Suitable stiff wooden objects include: logs, saplings, and model-cum-actresses. Cover these with a thick layer of dry, windproof thatch, such as that found on Tony Blackburn's head.

Secure your camp against the invasion of small, aggravating ants.
And even smaller, equally aggravating Decs. Ant and Dec are parasites indigenous to all Reality TV Shows. Regrettably, no satisfactory chemical method has yet been found for eliminating them.

Attempt to communicate with your fellow hostages: try to ascertain whether any of them speak English.
This is unlikely to be the case – bearing in mind that your fellow hostages are the aforementioned washed-up radio

DJs, sports personalities and unemployed model-cum-actresses.

If this fails, try instead to open a dialogue with your captors.

Repeatedly utter a few simple words of Geordie, such as, 'Why-aye man!', 'Areye alreet pet?' or 'Up the Toon Army!'

Be prepared for your captors to parade and humiliate you in front of the TV cameras as a warning to rival networks.

This tactic is frequently used by Saddam Hussein and other evil dictators.

If questioned, avoid revealing any more personal details than are absolutely necessary.

Keep your powder dry – and save this for the cash-in book, kiss and tell story or TV interview when you finally escape.

Give just the bare minimum of information: your name and celebrity rank.

E.g., 'My name is Darren, and I'm a D-list personality.'

Do all you can to attract the attention of small passing viewerships.

Wave, jump up and down and shout 'Over here, over here!' Rub two sticks together and start a fire. If this fails to raise the ratings, rub two celebrities together and start a lesbian relationship.

Menfolk in your camp should remain on Red Alert for potential Tara-wrist activity.
Male genitals may be a prime target for predatory It Girls, such as Ms Palmer-Tompkinson.

If your predicament becomes increasingly uncomfortable, you may have to resort to eating human flesh.
Close your eyes, open your mouth and clamp your jaws round the soft fleshy parts of your fellow hostage's body. The parts inside his pants will prove particularly tasty to the tabloid press, resulting in your being labelled a Celebrity Slapper and voted out early.

If unlucky, you may be forced into a forfeit by your fellow nonentities.
This could include involuntary swallowing of a maggot. If you are a Celebrity Slapper (see above), this should present no difficulty whatsoever.

Try to prevent yourself from becoming painfully thin, gaunt and skeletal during your ordeal.
Unless you are also planning to enter the reality show *Model Behaviour*.

In hot climates, thirst will inevitably be a problem. Avoid drinking the water from puddles or stagnant pools, which may harbour dangerous bacteria.
Instead, curb your raging thirst until the cameras are turned away. Then avail yourself of the free bottles of Evian passed

round by the production staff (along with the cigarettes, chocolate bars, Big Macs, scented napkins, moistened toilet tissue and selection of dry-roasted nuts from the neighbouring four-star hotel's minibar).

If any of your party has a mobile telephone, use this to summon assistance.
Dial the *Survivor* eviction hotline and vote yourself out. Repeat until the battery is drained of power.

Remember that your kidnapping is nothing more than a cowardly attempt to extort money. When your captors have attained their financial objective, you will probably be released entirely unharmed.
At £1.50 per minute, this should only take a few million calls to the Eviction Hotline.

When voted out of the Survivor camp, seek cover without delay.
Seeking the cover of *The Sun*, *The Mirror* or *The Daily Star* will ensure maximum publicity.

Warning: after two weeks in the jungle, you may be suffering from extreme overexposure.
If people seem to be physically sick of you, lie low for a few days before venturing back into the public eye.

Do not proceed immediately to a qualified doctor.
Proceed to an unqualified doctor, such as 'Doctor' Neil Fox, who is an expert in desperate cases of Post Reality-show

Appearance Traumatisation Syndrome (or P.R.A.T.S.). Your public profile may also benefit from several therapeutic sessions on the pastel-coloured couch with Richard and Judy.

Take preventative measures to stop yourself being targeted by future series of *I'm a Celebrity, Get Me Out Of Here!*

You can do this by becoming a *real* bona fide celebrity, as opposed to a third-rate showbiz wannabe who people vaguely recognise from having been in The Priory with a drink problem.

How To Wear A Skimpy Bikini

To limit the risk of permanent emotional scarring, wait if possible for optimum Bikini-wearing conditions.

In Britain, this means a temperature above 60 degrees Fahrenheit, wind-speed below Gale Force 7 and hailstones less than 0.5 inches in diameter. Keep an emergency kit containing your Bikini, some clean towels and a bucket (and/or spade) ready-packed for immediate departure – suitable clothing take-off windows only arise once every two or three years and may last just 48 hours.

Before you attempt to put on the Bikini, familiarise yourself with the anatomical parts you are about to inflict on the general public.

Obtain an independent assessment from a trusted friend or colleague. Is your body more *Baywatch* or *Crimewatch*?

Remember that indecent exposure is a serious crime in most European countries.

If you are in Holland, disregard this warning.

Stand up straight and direct the eyes downward. Do you notice a prominent fleshy protrusion extending outward by approximately eight inches?

If not, proceed immediately to the final stage. Otherwise continue to the next step.

Do you wish that this fleshy protrusion were (a) larger or (b) smaller?

If (a), you are a bloke. Please abandon the Bikini-wearing procedure immediately. It will be better for all concerned. If you are rampantly homosexual and determined to show off your bod on the beach, at least show some decorum and wear the standard gay apparel of a skin-diving wetsuit with a large circle of Lycra cut out of the buttock area.

If (b), you are a woman. The fleshy protrusion is your stomach.

Proceed immediately to the beach, but DO NOT attempt to put on the Bikini.

Put on enough warm layers of clothing for a major Arctic expedition.

Approach the water's edge with care.

Wear dark glasses to protect your eyes from the bright white glare of other pasty-skinned Brits ill advisedly wearing Bikinis, and/or threadbare swimming trunks which make their genitalia resemble a small string bag of kumquats.

DO NOT bathe where you see a Blue Flag flying.

A Blue Flag indicates that the water is within acceptable standards of pollution. Fortunately, such areas are rarely encountered in this country.

Take a deep breath and immerse your entire head in the water.

If you open your eyes, you will see the myriad of rare and beautiful indigenous fauna which inhabit our marine coastlines. Such as *Ejaculus Durex* (the Used Condom), *Excreta Humungus* (the Massive Floating Turd) and *Toxicara Illegala* (the non EC-compliant Industrial Effluent Byproduct).

When you can hold your breath no longer, come up for air.
Swill a little of the seawater around in your mouth. Swallow as much as you can. Try not to spit, even if you find the salty taste unpleasant.

Return to your hotel, car or beach hut.
You should now have succeeded in contracting dysentery, typhoid, cholera or another serious water-borne disease.

Vomit repeatedly and lose four stone in weight.
Now put your Bikini on.

Return to the beach.
Do not drop your guard. If you see a group of people in ponchos approaching at speed with a large net and banners reading 'Save the Beached Whale', retreat immediately and remove the Bikini without delay.

How To Remove A Skimpy Bikini

1) From Yourself

Run to a place of privacy, like a beach hut, windbreak, behind a large rocky outcrop or sunbathing Fat Bastard.
If necessary, seize a bucket and spade from the nearest infant and dig yourself a protective hole in the sand.

Grit your teeth against the pain.
Your movements may be restricted by tight nylon strings cutting deep into your flesh.

Try to insert one or two fingers under the least tight of these restrictive ligatures.
If this is not physically possible, insert one or two fingers down your throat and try to puke up all the 99 Flake ice creams you've been stuffing your fat face with. Your Bikini may now feel slightly looser.

Lubricate the area around the Bikini straps. This will make the bindings easier to wriggle out of.
Suitable emollient should not be difficult to come by. You will find a large drum of diesel oil bobbing about in the water

of any British beach. If no drum is available, simply wipe some oil off the nearest dead seagull or guillemot.

Inhale deeply. Hold your breath as though preparing for a deep-sea dive.
Scuba equipment is optional.

Contract the stomach muscles.
Rotate the Bikini to loosen it. Attempt to free yourself from the taut bonds by swivelling your torso repeatedly clockwise and anticlockwise through 45 degrees.

If the Bikini is too tight to remove by the rotation method, look around for a serrated object or cutting blade.
A sharp-edged shell will suffice, but a razor blade abandoned on the beach by some local smack addicts will be more effective. These should be readily available.

Carefully slit the Bikini straps to release your flabby thighs.
Be careful not to slit your flabby thighs in the process, unless you are a qualified plastic surgeon.

Repeat the process on the upper portion of the Bikini.
You may wish to have a hammock or deckchair on hand to catch your breasts when you release them.

Wipe the skin with a swab to remove any remaining traces of biologically hazardous material.

Unless you wish to sport that deep brown, all-over tan – in which case simply spray your entire torso with aerosol deodorant to remove the lingering odour of human waste produce.

Cover the exposed flesh immediately with suitable dressings.

For example, a brightly-coloured sarong, Union Jack pants, 'My Mate Went To Skeggy And All I Got Was This Lousy T-Shirt' T-shirt and Rayban Aviators (fake). Or other appropriate items of British touristwear.

2) From Your Female Companion

Stand well back from the Bikini wearer.

View her from a safe distance, with your eyes narrowed and your head tilted to one side to denote deep concentration.

Wait for her to ask whether the Bikini makes her look fat.

This will occur after approximately five seconds.

Answer in the affirmative.

Be prepared for an eruption of anger.

Retreat to a safe distance until your female companion has accomplished the Bikini removal procedure, as described above.

Observe her carefully. If she is using her sharp serrated object or razor blade to make an incision in her wrists (and not her Bikini straps), gently withdraw your comment about her fatness and pour flattering comments on the affected area (e.g., her bum).

CHAPTER FOUR

Survival In The Workplace

How To Survive A Random Outbreak Of Firing

Random firing can occur without warning in hostile, uncivilised environments, such as the modern corporate office.

In the event of being caught up in the bloodbath, you can salvage some modicum of dignity by following the procedure outlined below.

When the firing starts, grab as many personal items as you can from your desk.

Take only the things most precious to you, such as the photo of your spouse, photo of your children, expensive Personal Digital Assistant, attractive 19-year-old Secretarial Assistant.

Get down low on the ground.

Grovelling to your boss may convince him or her to change their mind about firing you.

Warn colleagues about oncoming redundancies.

Shout 'Everybody out of here!' Try to get all your workmates to evacuate the building (if the entire workforce is sacked, you won't feel so crap about your own dismissal).

Raise the alarm by smashing the glass to sound the Fire Bell.

Locate the fire extinguisher and release the safety catch. Squirt the foam liberally over your ex-boss to smother their ugly face. Ensure that he or she is well put out.

Run to a phone and dial the first premium-rate sex line you can find. Be sure not to position the receiver carefully back on the cradle.
Repeat with all phones in the building.

Exit the premises, safe in the knowledge that you no longer work there and will thus escape retribution for running up a £500-a-minute telephone bill.
Do not return to the scene of the firing unless equipped with a protective suit (i.e. one for Unfair Dismissal on the grounds of Sexism/Racism/Anti-Semitism/Size-ism/Ageism/Crap Worker-ism).

How To Deal With A Stockmarket Crash Victim

Wait until prices have finished falling.
A charging bear market can be dangerously unpredictable. Your first concern should be for your own safety and fiscal wellbeing.

Feel the victim's arms, legs and torso for any large bumps or swellings.
You are trying to find a purse, even a shallow or barely discernible one.

If you do locate a purse or wallet, remove it immediately and perform a cash injection into the victim's bank account.
The victim may be carrying an Organ Donor card. Discard this and search instead for a Diners Club card, Gold Amex or Visa/Mastercard.

Check for any badly brokered deals, and close vulnerable financial positions as soon as possible.
If the victim is conscious, speak to them and reassure them that an economic upturn is just around the corner.

Follow the standard procedure for treating Insolvency-Abuse victims.

Try to reduce bank-withdrawal symptoms. Caution! Do not allow the victim to sink deeper into debt: stay with them and talk them out of doing any stupid deals. The victim is severely financially unstable and should not be left a loan.

Can you see any angry red marks beginning to appear, e.g., on brown envelopes headed 'Final Demand', 'Penalty Due' and 'Urgent Action Required'?

This indicates a worsening of the monetary situation. Phone a qualified Financial Adviser immediately.

If too much money is bleeding from the bank account, try to massage the figures, using an Andersen Consultant if necessary. If professional help is unavailable, drive the victim to the nearest major trading centre (Canary Wharf, Wall Street, Hong Kong). Keep checking their portfolios at regular intervals. Try to get as high up as possible (to the top floor of the HSBC Tower).

At greater altitudes, the air is clearer and the victim may be capable of more rational thought.

Open all windows to facilitate the flow of suicidal traders. Stay with the victim until they are physically strong enough to jump off the window ledge by themselves.

Collect their life insurance. As explained above, your immediate concern in financially threatening situations is for your OWN security.

Remortgage to a safe extent, and wait for the economy to adopt the Recovery Position (indicated by the presence of green shoots).

How To Break Into The Modelling Industry

Be prepared for a tough task. The modelling world is notoriously difficult to gain entry into.

Consider breaking into something easier, like Fort Knox or the Bank of England. Both are a more straightforward prospect, although not quite so financially lucrative.

Before you attempt to break into the Modelling Industry, equip yourself with the correct tools for the job.

You will need: a coat hanger (bent into the shape of a coat hanger) and a small pair of tweezers suitable for lock picking or eyebrow plucking. A small compact mirror can also be used to focus the sun's rays and light a ciggie, though it is more useful for checking your mascara.

Before you attempt to break into modelling, strap something made of inflatable rubber material around your chest.

Such as breast implants.

Proceed to a remote, windswept location, preferably near a magnificent rolling ocean or some suitably picturesque mountains.

Sooner or later, a deputation of glossy magazine employees will turn up to do a needlessly expensive fashion shoot.

Take no food or drink. The weaker you appear, the greater your chances of being snapped up.

If you begin to feel the cold, light a fag by rubbing one cancer-stick against a lighter. You should be able to survive on 50 or 60 cigarettes a day.

Wriggle out of any restrictive bra-straps or drawstring trousers.

Allow the breasts to swing freely in the open air. They can be used to swish away bloodsucking insects and other predators. Large bazookas are invaluable for self-defence.

Scan the surrounding area for signs of freshly picked bones, human remains or decomposing corpses.

These are your fellow models. Kill them. (Warning! Enraged models may bite or scratch if provoked!) Alternatively, just wait for them to starve to death or snuff it from a drug-overdose.

Refrain from eating for at least three weeks. If you come across any edible plants or animals, employ willpower to resist eating them and remain on a strict no-calorie diet.

This will facilitate squeezing into small apertures, such as the waistband of a size 6 pencil skirt.

Should hunger pangs become unbearable, you may have to resort to eating one of your own limbs.

This will assist you in rapid weight loss of at least 6–8lb

(arm) or 12–14lb (leg), provided you vomit it up afterwards. Caution! Only adopt this tactic if the asymmetrical look is currently fashionable.

Remain vigilant. You may be approached by headhunters, who will attempt to shrink your body and put you on the cover of Vogue.

If you suspect you are being watched, adopt a grumpy pout and apply fresh warpaint to areas of exposed skin.

Wear unsuitable clothing.

Steel toe-capped desert boots, khaki combat trousers, an ammunition belt and a flak jacket are also ideal if accessorised with a floaty chiffon scarf for the summer's essential Military Chic look.

Ensure your footwear is both (a) uncomfortable and (b) impractical.

Chafing shoes are essential in order to maintain the surly, pained expression of the successful supermodel.

Identify a long strip of clear, unbroken ground, suitable for use as a runway.

Shift any excess stones from the surrounding area. Also shift any excess stones from your midriff area. Proceed down the runway with your stomach muscles contracted, your chin pointing in an upward direction and a glassy-eyed expression. DO NOT under any circumstances try to break into a smile.

Maintain a steady velocity until your modelling career takes off.

If your career is not progressing quickly enough, administer intravenous drugs. Doing so in the company of the right people will greatly increase your job prospects. Continue taking the drugs until your therapist certifies you to be in a suitably unstable condition.

If you still haven't broken into the Modelling Industry, consider changing the locks.

Change your locks to several shades blonder. Fashion Editors are often vulnerable to being struck by lightening. If this doesn't work, stick your fingers in an electric socket to avoid the expense of a perm.

In extreme circumstances, you may have to perform a manual jerk-off.

Approach the photographer or model booker in a well-lit area, such as a studio in Soho. Using maximum forward thrust, engage his interest by releasing your flaps. Use the button located above his trouser zipper to operate his undercarriage. If he is already 'flying low', this procedure should be easily accomplished.

Prepare to go down.

Pull the ripcord to remove your lingerie, and ensure that the legs are able to open unobstructed.

Cling tightly to your partner and warn him to prepare for a bumpy ride.

After pressing the Ejaculate button, hold tight until motion has stopped and you have come to rest.

Doors into the Modelling World should now have opened for you.

If you still experience problems, the difficulty may be a physical one. Consult a neurosurgeon, who should be able to solve the problem by means of a simple brain removal or frontal lobotomy. Facial reconstructive surgery may also help if you are exceptionally unattractive.

Warning! When breaking *into* modelling, bear in mind that you must never break *out* in spots.

How To Rob A Bank

This is a useful skill to master if you need to survive a financial crisis, or simply wish to get on television without the embarrassment of applying to be on Big Brother.

Ensure, however, that when robbing the Bank you collect enough money for the airfare to a country where you can claim political asylum. Brazil is very nice, I hear.

Select your target.

Choose a Bank against which you have a particular grudge. If you were recently charged £25 for a letter informing you that your account was 38p overdrawn, or if the cashier put up their Position Closed sign just before you got to the window last Friday lunchtime, either of these may be put forward in a Court of Law as evidence of extreme provocation.

You will need:
A gun
A big bag
Two pairs of clean underwear (one to wear on your nether regions, one to wear over your head for disguise purposes).

Case the joint.

The precise meaning of this is unclear, but people in Bank Robber Films seem to say it a lot so it must be important. It would probably be a good idea to look for large amounts of money just lying around unguarded, or big steel vaults with the door swinging wide open.

Wear a mask.

You can obtain a clown mask from any good joke shop. If you are subsequently spotted, eyewitness statements will lead to Ronald MacDonald being pulled in for questioning. And he can obviously afford to pay back all the loot.

Approach a cashier, and ask her for all her money.

She will probably ask you to provide your chequebook and card, sort code number and two forms of identification, like a recent utility bill. She is bluffing. You do not need to produce these fiddly and difficult-to-obtain items. Producing a gun will suffice.

Take the cash.

If you are asked how you would like it, specify hundred or fifty pound notes. Do not specify fifty pence pieces, unless you have a very large sack and a lot of time on your hands.

Get out, fast.

If you see a large number of policemen outside, try to look like a normal Bank customer. Hide the money (and the gun) and adopt a pissed-off expression, muttering darkly about cashiers who take three-hour lunchbreaks from 11 a.m. onwards.

If your disguise is rumbled, take evasive action.

Wave your gun around in a threatening fashion. The police may try to grab it. This is because they are jealous due to not having any guns of their own. Remain calm and try not to shoot anybody, since this reflects badly on you if you get taken to court.

Do not count your money straight away.

People rarely count large sums of money when standing around in the vicinity of a recent Bank Job. If you cannot contain your enthusiasm to count your loot, pretend you are the chairman of a large public utility. You can do this by producing two recent utility bills and explaining, 'I am the Chairman of British Gas/Yorkshire Water.'

If you get caught, destroy this Book.

The Author does not wish to be implicated as an accessory to violent crime. If you get away with it, however, donations are welcome c/o the Publishers and would be a nice gesture of your appreciation.

How To Escape From A Maximum Security Jail

If you have successfully followed the previous instructions (see: 'How To Rob A Bank') this may be particularly pertinent to your situation.

Assess the situation in a level-headed way.

Are you a corporate fraudster, celebrity gangster whose life has been immortalised in a book and/or film, or disgraced former Peer of the Realm with a predilection for leaving money in luggage lockers at Victoria Station? If so, abandon your escape attempt. Your life in jail will be comparable to a stay in a five-star hotel. Consider duffing up a screw to get your sentence extended by 18 months or so.

If you are NOT in a cushy Open Jail, read on.

You will need:
    A small spoon
    An enormous amount of free time.
None of these should be difficult to come by. If your sentence expires before your escape attempt has been accomplished, do not follow the above advice about duffing up a screw to get your sentence extended by 18 months or so. That would be silly.

First, try to exit via the door.

You may be in luck. If Group Four manages your jail, you

will simply be able to stroll out when and how you please. If the door is locked, check that there isn't a large bunch of keys in the lock or hanging from the back of the door on a bit of string.

In the unlikely event that the door is locked, locate a weak spot in the wall of your cell.

It is best not to pick a supporting wall if you prefer not to be crushed by falling rubble.

Scrape the spoon firmly against the wall of the cell and remove any debris.

Repeat several hundred million times.

A hole of increasingly large diameter should gradually appear in the wall.

To avoid alerting the unwanted attention of the Prison Warders, be sure to conceal the hole with your bedstead, your slopping-out bucket, or the big bag of pure Colombian cocaine which your visitors brought you.

Find out what's on the other side of the hole.

If the genitalia of the inmate next door come poking through it, abandon your escape attempt and try digging through another wall at 90 degrees to the first one. If there is a window in the wall looking out on some rolling green fields, this is possibly a clue as to which wall would be the best choice for digging through.

Keep your strength up for your escape attempt by consuming plenty of prison food.

Do not use the same spoon as you have used for digging through the cement. You may break your spoon by attempting to penetrate some prison sponge-pudding, and jeopardize your chances of successfully absconding.

Try to lose weight, so that you can slip more easily through a small hole in the wall.
OK, forget what I just said about consuming plenty of prison food.

Before you escape, put a dummy in your bed so that nobody notices you're not in it.
An inflatable sex-doll, shop window model or tailors' mannequin are all easily obtainable, though perhaps less so when you're banged up in Strangeways. If none of these are available to you, improvise using a full laundry bag, a very large poo from your slop bucket, or a recently murdered cellmate.

When the aperture is large enough to squeeze your entire body through, squeeze your entire body through it.
Now run. Fast. Especially if there are lots of alarm bells going off.

If you are unlucky, the hole will only lead into the exercise yard. If this is the case, make sure you retain your spoon in order to dig a tunnel under the perimeter wall.
The ideal tunnel should be no fewer than ten feet in depth. You should be able to dig this in approximately ten to fifteen

years, depending on the capacity of the spoon. Conveniently enough, this is roughly the same amount of time you will have added to your original sentence as a punishment for breaking out of your cell.

Savour your freedom.
Use your spoon to make yourself a nice cup of tea, although do not be surprised if it tastes a bit gravelly.

How To Deal With A Charging Credit Card

Try to remain calm. When approached for a minimum 5 per cent payment to be received on or before the 31st, do not shout or scream.

Such crippling demands are perfectly normal. If you are a woman, you will be bled dry by your credit card company at the same time every month, although the heaviness of cashflow may vary.

Using a clean, sharp object, make a firm incision to the middle of the credit card and draw the blade from one side to the other. This should relieve excessive spending.

If you are particularly squeamish about money, it may be easier to get someone else to wield the blade.

Wait for your swollen monthly demands to gradually return to more normal proportions. Remember! Even once your finances have recovered, your credit rating may still be dangerously low.

Do not make any sudden purchases, which may cause a relapse or irreversible fiscal handicap.

If fits of overspending run in your family, be prepared for an early overdraft. Accept that you may lose some of your friends as a result of your restricted financial circumstances – debt is a natural process that comes to us all at some point.

(Normally at the end of University Life).

How To Spot A Lying Politician

When the politician extends their arm for a handshake, grasp their hand and press your thumb gently but firmly below the wrist joint.

If you can feel a pulse, continue your examination. If you cannot feel a pulse, the politician is probably a member of the House of Lords and therefore already clinically dead. He or she no longer poses a threat.

Observe the politician's face. Are the lips moving, teeth visible, or jaws opening and closing repeatedly? Is any sound issuing from the voicebox?

The politician is lying. Run for your life.

Do not take refuge in any empty shed-like structures.

This may turn out to be a polling booth. If confronted by a ballot paper, do not attempt to vote. Swallow the ballot paper and make your exit as rapidly as possible.

How To Climb A Greasy Pole

Assess the situation in a level-headed fashion. First discern whether you are a man or a woman.

For an indication of your gender, look carefully at your trouser area. If you can identify a prominent bulge or protrusion, this confirms that you are a man (and have just pocketed a big wodge of money in your annual bonus).

If you are NOT a man, get to hospital as quickly as possible and undergo a sex-change operation.

Now return to the workplace, where you will find your progress unhindered by the physical handicap of having breasts.

Identify the Alpha Male in your corporate environment.

He will be the one with silvery hair, which may or may not be a toupee, and will be asserting his authority by sleeping off a four-hour liquid lunch or swearing at his computer.

Try to corner the Alpha Male (or MD) in his natural environment.

This will take persistence and dedication. He may retreat away from the workplace and hide in a bunker at a private Golf Club in Hampshire: you will know this because his secretary will try to deflect your approach by informing you that 'Mr Felchingham is on a course for three weeks and cannot be disturbed!'

Track down the MD by following the trail of crap he leaves for his underlings to deal with. When you locate him, try to gain his trust by performing the universally recognised tribal friendship signal. Roll up your trouser leg and expose your left nipple.

Pick up a large, blunt object (such as a 9-iron) and hit the golf ball as hard as you can with the heavy end. If this demonstration of golfing prowess does not mark you out as management material, pick up the same Nine Iron and hit your MD as hard as you can with the heavy end. Whilst he's off sick, clear his desk for him and apply for his job.

How to Disguise The Fact That You Are The Only Person In The Office Not To Find *Frasier* Funny

Avoid all Frasier*-related conversations where possible.*

Check regularly in newspapers and TV listings magazines. If you spot a particularly 'hilarious' forthcoming episode on Friday, consider taking Monday off work to escape subsequent repetition of every single joke by your colleagues in a bad American accent.

Learn to recognise a Frasier *fan before they have a chance to engage you in conversation.*

Key signs include: consumption of more than ten cups of American-style coffee per day. Slight Seattle drawl and/or unconvincing Mancunian dialect when speaking. Receding hair. Unavailability for social events on a Friday night. Continually asking you whether you wish to talk about your problems and use of the phrase 'I'm listening,' even when they're not.

If evading a Frasier*-related conversation is physically impossible, use your skill and cunning to feign a mirthful response.*

Ardent *Frasier* devotees are generally simple creatures and can be easily tricked into believing you are one of their own.

Adopt a knowledgeable smile when the subject of Frasier *is mentioned.*

When you see the *Frasier* fans draw back their lips and bare their teeth in a broad grin, mimic their reactions. Pivot the head in a repeated up-and-down motion, intoning 'Oh yeah!' or 'That was a good one!'

Inhale deeply. Fill your lungs with sufficient air to produce a loud volley of laughter.

Do not emit the laugh until a particularly brilliant joke is recalled. This may alert the *Frasier* fans to the fact that you are an impostor.

Brace yourself to deliver the Guffaw. Timing is crucial – your laugh must coincide with mention of something exquisitely comedic involving Eddie the dog or Niles' sex life.

You can identify the optimum laughing point by the *Frasier* fans appearing to go into spasm. Their shoulders will shake, rapidly developing into a state of semi-paralysis that affects the entire face and body. Those most severely affected may collapse to the floor, or be incapable of standing up without holding on to furniture. Their breathing will become irregular and flecks of spit may be showered from their mouths. Stand well away from such chronic cases, since their Frasiermania may be contagious and they may pass on a book or video to you.

Deliver the laugh, aiming it in a 'scattergun' pattern at each of the Frasier *fans in succession.*
Open your mouth, ensuring the airway is clear of such obstructions as phlegm, vomit, or unmasticated boluses of food, which may be propelled out by the force of the laugh. Tense the muscles at the back of your larynx, then release a lungful of air in synchronicity with the supposed 'punchline'. Repeat this process several times to produce a staccato 'ha-ha-ha' sound. Place the palms of the hands flat against the ribs, pointing upwards and exerting a slight pressure on the ribcage, bending forward at the waist as though about to suffer imminent loss of all physical coordination. You may also wish to dribble a little at this point.

When the laughter subsides, make your excuses and leave.
Do not remain in the vicinity, or you may be interrogated about your favourite episode ever or drawn into difficult questions about whether American sitcoms are superior to their British equivalent.

Get to a telephone, and immediately contact a registered psychotherapist or local radio shrink.
These people are qualified in Freudian analytical techniques, and over a period of months should be able to cure you of your irrational failure to piss yourself laughing every time Frasier *is on.*

HOW TO DISGUISE THE FACT THAT YOU ARE THE ONLY PERSON IN THE OFFICE NOT TO FIND *FRASIER* FUNNY

NB: The aforementioned technique may also be applied to *Friends, Ali G, The Fast Show, Monty Python* and *Sex and the City* (but not *Hale and Pace* or *The Brian Conley Show*, to which laughter is not a socially acceptable response even under extreme emergency circumstances).

CHAPTER FIVE

Surviving Sport and Leisure Activities

How To Save A Test Match

Assess the situation in a rational manner. At this stage, it is unlikely that a win will be within your reach.

Rescuing a Test Match is inevitably a salvage operation or damage-limitation exercise.

Be responsible.

Throwing away matches in hot, dry, foreign climates is very thoughtless behaviour. It is best not to dispose of any Ashes in areas such as Australia, but to take them back home with you.

However scared you might be, try not to soil your trousers.

Filling your pockets with soil will leave you dangerously exposed to accusations of Ball Tampering.

Wear protective apparel.

During the English summer, a sou'wester and oilskins are recommended. If these are forbidden by the Umpire, shinpads and a cricket box are vital to protect your vulnerable extremities. Pay particular attention to the Googlies. A wounded tail-end is very painful!

When visiting areas known for their dangerous natives (such as Melbourne), be sure to carry an offensive weapon at all times.

A large, blunt, wooden object shaped like a Cricket Bat is ideal. A didgeridoo or boomerang is less useful.

Locate a long strip of wide open grassland, roughly similar in size to an airfield.

Do not attempt to land a small plane or microlight on it. It may ruin the wicket by churning up the grass with its landing gear.

Travel in large groups of eleven or more.

Do not allow members of your party to stray from the hotel, or go out on the piss.

If members of your party are injured, get to a TV camera immediately and deploy the 'Flintoff's Groin' excuse.

Early deployment of weak excuses may limit your embarrassment when you eventually lose by an innings and 356 runs.

Find a suitable wooden outbuilding (or Pavilion) and formulate a logical plan of attack.
Then abandon it.

Accept the fact that you are likely to be very badly beaten.
In areas such as Australia, it is common for tourists to be given a complete mauling in Big Game situations.

Identify two short wooden sticks, such as a resourceful Bushman might rub together to start a fire.
DO NOT rub them together to start a fire, even if you are desperate to take home the Ashes. Place the two sticks horizontally on top of three vertical sticks. Ensure they are well balanced.

Sticky pith or sap from a gum-tree may be employed to glue the two sticks (or 'bails') firmly in position.
But only if the Umpire has his back turned.

Stand at the 'Crease', shielding your delicate groin region by holding your blunt wooden artefact directly in front of you.
Accept that you are an easy target for bloodthirsty Spinners, who invariably attack groups of weak English tourists by throwing small, hard, spherical objects at them.

If you see a small, hard, spherical object approaching you at high velocity, try to deflect it with your blunt piece of wood.

Do not turn around and run away from the scene until AFTER you've hit the spherical object.

Run as fast as you can in a straight line.

Zigzagging from side to side or doubling-back on yourself will cause confusion. Especially to your own team-mates.

Remember that you are in an area of international conflict which may have been designated an official Disaster Zone. However, getting out as quickly as possible should NOT be your primary consideration.

It is far more important to think about staying in.

Remain vigilant. Use all your skill and resourcefulness to avoid being caught by hostile Fielders, who may lurk in the Slips waiting to catch unwary Englishmen.

If you are caught by a member of the opposing team, stand as still as you can. Do not run away. Do not walk. Demand a review of video evidence from the Third Umpire.

Beware of falling wickets!

These can often cause fatal bruising to your pride. If you hear someone shout 'Duck!', do not crouch down to dodge flying shrapnel. They are merely referring to your having posted a big fat 0 on the scoreboard.

Only retreat back to the pavilion when you have been comprehensively slaughtered.

Remain alert for other hazards. Do not stop on the way when ambushed by hostile TV commentary teams.

You should now resort to Plan B, in an attempt to salvage a draw.

Stand outside the pavilion and jerk your limbs around in a haphazard fashion. You are performing a Rain Dance to summon up the benevolent God of English Summer. If you are fortunate, he may smile upon you and consent to make it piss down before the final day of the Test.

Do not run for cover.

Leave this to the groundsmen. They will install the covers over the pitch, thereby saving your men from suffering further heavy losses.

How To Avoid Being Stuck Behind A Big-Haired Person In The Cinema

1) In A Horror Film

Politely ask the Big-Haired Person to move.
This request will naturally be ignored.

During the trailers, vacate the cinema via the Emergency Exit.
Locate your nearest hardware store and purchase a cordless chainsaw or set of powerful hedge-trimmers. Select the most expensive you can afford; the additional expense will still come to less than the cost of the cinema tickets.

Return to your seat.
The auditorium will now be in darkness. A wise filmgoer will have purchased a torch, flashlight, orienteering beacons and stout leather hiking boots from the hardware store to facilitate safe return to Row 4B. Ensure that you annoy as many fellow cinemagoers as possible by asking them to stand up and let you pass.

Stare at the back of the Big-Haired Person's head until the action reaches a suitably gory point.
This is signified by the screams of female audience members in response to male audience members attempting to use

their partners' fear as an excuse for putting an arm around her shoulders and unsubtly groping her breasts.

Remove your chainsaw from its packaging and engage the cutting mechanism.

Using a bold, sideways swipe, sever the offending hairdo at the root of the follicles. The sound of the screaming should drown out any mechanical noise.

If your view of the film remains impeded, sever the head of the Big-Haired Person at the base of the shoulder blades.

This should not attract suspicion; fellow filmgoers will merely assume it is some exciting new interactive element of the Horror Film Experience.

Sit back and view the film in comfort.

You now have an unhindered view of the screen, and no longer need worry about the person in front of you complaining that you've just dropped popcorn down the back of their neck.

2) In An Adult Film

Before entering the auditorium, ensure that your have equipped yourself with suitable provisions.

You will require an Ice Lolly, a thick banana milkshake and a drinking straw. A six-gallon industrial-sized bucket of banana milkshake will be available from the Refreshment Kiosk. Obtain one by asking for a 'Small Shake, please'.

Take up your seat behind the Big-Haired Person.

Try to ignore the over-amorous courting couple behind you who will already be having sex even though the most titillating thing on screen so far is Mr Raj from the Bengal Tiger Tandoori advertising his sizzling Prawn Bhuna available 'just 300 yards from this film house.'

When the film commences, begin sucking your Ice Lolly as loudly as you can.

Express your satisfaction with repeated 'mmmm, mmmm' noises. It is not strictly necessary to actually ingest any of the Ice Lolly. If you are prone to hyperactivity or additive-related psychiatric disorders you may prefer not to.

Place your Ice Lolly to one side.

Try to avoid dropping it into the lap of a neighbouring audience member, unless the neighbouring audience member is single, male, middle-aged and already showing visible signs of sexual arousal.

Insert your drinking straw into your Thick Banana Shake and apply your lips to the open end of the straw.

Suck firmly, creating a vacuum inside the straw. However, do not allow any milkshake to enter your mouth. Place the tongue over the top of the straw to seal the aperture and hold the milkshake inside it.

Keeping the tongue safely over the aperture, remove the straw from the milkshake bucket and aim it in the direction of the Big-Haired Person's neck.

Maintain this posture until the on-screen action enters a steamier phase.

Using as much lungpower as you can muster, blow on the straw to propel the thick banana milkshake out of the straw at high velocity. Accompany this with a groan of 'Ooh yeah'.

If the projectile milkshake fails to impact on the Big-Haired Person, repeat the process with greater accuracy.

Allow several seconds for the Big-Haired Person to rationally assess the situation.

The Big-Haired Person will naturally conclude that a male audience member in the row behind is thoroughly enjoying the film.

The Big-Haired Person should now vacate his or her seat.

Either they will run out of the auditorium in disgust, or they will move back one row in order to join in. Both eventualities will ensure that you now have a clear line of sight to the cinema screen. (NB: For those in a long-term relationship who wish to save themselves the cost of a Thick Banana Milkshake, the same result can be accomplished by actually performing sordid hand jobs during the film. If the Big-Haired Person complains, simply point out that human semen is rich in Vitamin E and works as a highly effective conditioner on dry scalps.)

3) In A Liz Hurley Film

Remain in your seat for two minutes after the film has commenced.
The Big-Haired Person will now have left, as will everyone else in the cinema. Your view of the screen is now entirely unobstructed.

Pursue the Big-Haired Person.
Being on foot, he or she will hopefully not have had time to get very far from the scene.

Offer the Big-Haired Person a monetary reward if they will return to their seat to block your view of the film.
Employ brute force if necessary. As a last resort, wind a scarf or bandanna around your eyes, or shield your vision using an airline sleep mask. If you do witness more than five minutes of Ms Hurley's 'acting', seek professional trauma counselling and be prepared for many years of psychological torment.

How To Survive A Karaoke Christmas Party

Stay exactly where you are. Make no sudden, jerky movements, which could be misinterpreted as 'boogying'.

Do not venture towards the karaoke machine, even if you are familiar with how the controls work. Especially not if you are familiar with how the controls work.

Allow your colleagues to open hailing frequencies and transmit (on all available channels) the international Christmas Party Karaoke Distress Signal, otherwise known as Gloria Gaynor's 'I Will Survive'.

Protect your eardrums with cotton wool or earplugs. If neither is available, activate a Christmas cracker and utilise the paper hat contained within it. Retreat as far away from the karaoke machine as possible and assume a fixed grin.

Do not scream loudly or shout 'Help!'

This may backfire; you could find yourself dragged up to the microphone and urged to perform a Beatles duet with a goofy middle-manager wearing a pair of Deely Boppers and a sprig of mistletoe in his fly.

Close all doors and windows to prevent the music from contaminating a wider area.

Try to block or obstruct the karaoke victim's airway using a clenched fist, bauble, Quality Street toffee or overcooked Brussels sprout. If you can locate the office stapler, staple the victim's lips together.

Contact your corporate paymasters, ensuring that you provide chilling and incontrovertible evidence of how truly ghastly the Christmas piss-up has become.
Do this by sending them a single, recognisable bodily part. You could do this by photocopying your tits and faxing them to Head Office. Use of the Auto-Enlarge function is permissible but not compulsory.

Wearing rubber gloves (or in the case of a particularly debauched Office Party, rubber stockings and suspenders) use a pair of scissors from the stationery cupboard to cut the cable powering the karaoke machine.
If you have time, apologise to the two (or more) colleagues whose furtive shag in the stationery cupboard you have unwittingly interrupted.

Continue administering strong black coffee until the karaoke-er sobers up.
Destroy all karaoke CDs to prevent subsequent murder of classic rock tracks at a later date.

How To Feign Interest In Modern Art

Approach the Art with caution.

Warning! The Art may be in disguise. What may, on first examination, appear to be the result of someone vomiting after a particularly colourful curry could well turn out to be a load of old Jackson Pollocks.

HOW TO FEIGN INTEREST IN MODERN ART

Stand at least six feet away from the Art, facing in a forward direction.

Allow the Art to see that you aren't intimidated by it. Its eyes will probably follow you around the room. Remark to other gallery visitors on how incredible/marvellous/simply superb this is.

Place your hands behind your back and tilt your head to one side, adopting the 'enthralled' expression.

Hold this posture for at least 30 seconds. This will convey to your arty companions that you are not merely here to sample the particularly fine cappuccinos at the Tate Modern café, or because you've read in *GQ* that an art gallery is the latest place to pull hot totty.

Move in for a closer examination.

You may be required to fend off questions from fellow art aficionados. Their interrogation is designed to trick you into revealing yourself as an impostor. Your best policy is to remain silent, implying speechlessness as a result of exposure to such Great Art.

If unable to dodge oncoming questions, have some pre-prepared answers jotted down on the back of your hand.

Keep your wits about you. DO NOT, for instance, reply to questions about the quality of the light by poking the little lamp above the Art and saying you reckon a 60-Watt Soft-Tone bulb like you have in your lounge would have been much better.

Circle the Art, nodding several times and sucking air between your teeth in short sharp bursts to produce a 'tutting' sound.

This will assert your dominance as an Alpha Art Buff, and intimidate your fellow gallery visitors.

Try to identify whether the Artist is dangerous.

This will be indicated in the Programme, by such phrases as 'one of the more dangerous young British artists, an *enfant terrible* whose controversial video installation of his own proctology scan, entitled "Way Up My Own Arse", was a deserved winner of this year's Turner Prize.'

If the Art is not moving, do not be lulled into a false sense of security.

It is probably still worth more than your mortgage. You should remark at this point on how deeply, spiritually moving the Art is, even if it looks like something a five-year-old could have done (e.g., been sick on a canvas or piled some bricks in a corner).

Be careful to avoid tripping over any loose piles of bricks.

These may also be Art. However, do not compliment the pile of bricks on its sublimely transcending the boundaries between physical and metaphysical, in case it turns out to be something left behind by the builders when they built the new wing of the Tate Modern.

Expel the air from your lungs in a deep sigh.
This may be accompanied by a knowledgeable 'mmmmmmm'.

Move slowly and methodically around the gallery, occasionally returning to the same piece of Art for a second look, as though particularly captivated by it.
Remain quiet and reflective at all times. Refrain from comments such as 'God, that woman is such a lardarse!', either in reference to an original Reubens, or in reference to your fellow Art Lovers.

Remain alert at all times. You may see a large horned animal looming towards you.
Do not run, scream, or wave an item of scarlet-coloured clothing at it. Stay calm. It is merely a Damien Hirst. The animal will not attack, on account of its having been sliced in half, pickled in formaldehyde and stuck in a fish tank.

As you move around the gallery, try to stay in the centre of the room. Avoid situations where you can be cornered by Art Lovers and drawn into conversations about the Emerging Generation of Young Conceptualists.
If you hear a loud high-pitched whine, like the noise of an oncoming enemy aircraft, duck down and hide until the danger has passed. This will be Art Critic Brian Sewell.

As you leave each room, DO NOT switch off the lights.

They will switch off automatically as part of an award-winning postmodern installation entitled 'The Lights Go On And Off'.

Ensure that you complete the full circuit of the exhibition.

DO NOT succumb to the overwhelming urge to run from the scene, screaming with boredom.

Remark on how spiritually drained you feel after having been exposed to such breathtaking works.

However, do not demonstrate your exhaustion by lying down on a convenient but unmade bed. This, too, may be Art in disguise. Landing yourself with a £25,000 repair bill will not impress your Art-loving companions.

How To Survive A Barbecue

Identify a suitable area of open field or grassland, well away from residential buildings.

The ideal barbecuing spot should be free of trees and animals, and should be of sufficient size to land a light aircraft. Do not attempt to set up your barbecue in your living room or small family car.

Separate the men and women in your party. Instruct the female members of the group to remain indoors until given further notice.

This will prevent them interrupting your fire-making efforts with unwanted advice such as 'Why don't I just put the oven on?', 'Ainsley Harriot never does it like that' or 'Did you mean to set your hair alight?'

Remove raw meat from packaging.

Meat should have been previously obtained by scavenging around a local supermarket, using force where necessary to fight off rival shoppers. If you have neglected to locate fresh meat, scour your garden for small mammals (mouse, rat, stray cat, pet rabbit or guinea pig). If no suitable prey is available, you may have to sacrifice the weakest member of your group (civil servant, librarian, vegan) to provide protein-rich nourishment for the others.

Light the barbecue.

Make fire by rubbing two pieces of wood together. It is generally helpful if at least one of them is a match.

Ignite the charcoal briquettes. Charcoal briquettes can be found by scavenging your nearest 24-hour Petrol Station. They are often found between a set of L-plates, an out-of-date packet of lime-flavoured jelly and a *Now That's What I Call 1983* CD. Nobody is entirely sure why.

If your barbecue is alight, proceed to the cooking stage. If not, repeat the above processes until some idiot suggests pouring petrol on it.

Pour some petrol on it.

Pour some more petrol on it.

Go on, give it a good dousing. People are starving here.

Wave goodbye to your garden shed/attractive wooden patio furniture/eyebrows.

Your barbecue (and/or neighbour's fence) should now be burning nicely. Place the raw meat over the centre of the hot charcoal.

Remember, unwashed hands may contaminate the meat with dangerous bacteria. Other ways to contract food poisoning from your meat include leaving it in the sun for half an hour, dropping it on the patio or letting the cat get it. Food poisoning is an important element of any British barbecue, without which your al fresco eating experience will not be complete.

Whilst the meat is cooking, slice open several baps and hot dog rolls.

This is a decoy technique to create the impression that food is forthcoming. It will also allow the bread products to become sufficiently dry and unpalatable prior to consumption.

After a suitable period of cooking time (2–3 hours), relight your barbecue.

It will undoubtedly have extinguished itself 90 minutes ago without your noticing.

Severe hunger pangs are normal at this juncture. It is vital to keep up group morale! Despatch one member of your party indoors to ensure that your women are sufficiently lubricated.

One or more bottles of Chardonnay should be employed at this point. If no Chardonnay is available, you may improvise with the remainder of your lighter fluid. Failure to lubricate female guests may result in disastrous consequences such as sarcasm, nagging, or divorce proceedings.

Observe the first droplets of rain.

Even if it is the height of summer, a torrential downpour will now ensue.

Using a clean, sharp fork, make an incision into the soft fleshy part of one chicken leg. If bleeding is observed, replace the meat on the barbecue.

If no bleeding is observed, replace the meat on the barbecue. It is still frozen. (DO NOT be fooled into thinking it is cooked. Barbecue food can only exist in three states: frozen, raw, or incinerated to the point of resembling an ancient Roman artefact. None of these are known to be edible).

At this stage, brace yourself for someone to suggest getting a takeaway.

Using a clean, sharp fork, make an incision into the soft fleshy part of the offending person's stomach, This should be sufficient to halt further interjections.

HOW TO SURVIVE A BARBECUE

Distract your guests by creating a loud noise or other such diversionary tactic, such as a game of Twister.

Before your barbecue is completely extinguished, use the dying embers to send a smoke signal to your local tandoori restaurant, ordering chicken madras for ten and a dozen naan breads.

Repeat each summer.

CHAPTER SIX

Negotiating Perilous Social Minefields

How To Camouflage Your Inability To Cook

Proceed to your nearest supermarket and hunt down sufficient rations to feed a small army.
Be prepared to encounter dangerous wild animals in the process. Wild boar, ostrich, and kangaroo steaks are all popular with modern pretentious dinner party guests.

If necessary, engage in hand-to-hand combat to obtain the last remaining 350g serving of Chargrilled Marmoset and Wilted Roquette Filo Tartlettes With Wind-Dried Zucchini in the store.
A blunt object such as a bottle makes an effective weapon in such emergency situations. You should be able to obtain one from the Beer and Wine aisle, unless it is outside normal pub licensing hours.

Return home with your spoils.
Ensure that you allow at least three minutes (180 seconds)

preparation time prior to the commencement of your dinner party.

Remove the outer packaging, protective film and foil lids from your comestibles, as directed in the Serving Guidelines.

Attack your purchases using extreme physical violence. Punch, kick and pummel HomeStyle Chocolate Fudge cakes. Perform a karate chop on Minted Lamb Chops With Julienne Potatoes And A Piquant Cranberry Coulis. Using a sharp knife, make random stabbing motions at Finest Collection Summerfruit Pavlova. Shake thirty Mini Squat Lobster Vols-au-Vents until they are definitely dead. Grasp a ready-stuffed spatchcock chicken by the neck and use it to inflict severe bruising on a punnet of baby lychees.

If you feel your strength sapping, consume some of your provisions.

Do not consume too much, or your dinner party guests may perish from malnutrition.

Preheat your oven to 200 degrees Celsius or Gas Mark 6.

Whilst waiting for the oven to heat, shove everything in the microwave for five minutes.

Lubricate your skin with a little olive oil.

This will give the impression that you have been sweating profusely over the creation of your gourmet meal.

Open the oven door and insert your head until the skin attains a warm rosy glow.

This will also create the illusion of much strenuous exertion in the kitchen. Do not leave your head unattended in the oven until the skin becomes crispy and golden-brown (or dinner party guests will just think you've been sunning yourself in St Tropez.) If you have a gas oven, DO NOT inhale, however depressed you might be feeling about your impending role as Society Host/Hostess.

Wait for your guests to arrive.

If they are more than the fashionable 15 minutes late, send out additional invitations followed by a Red Cross search party.

Position a random selection of Trendy Cookbooks in prominent positions around your front room.

Place these directly in the path of toilet-bound diners, so your guests will be unable to avoid encountering them.

Seat your guests at the table.

Adhere strictly to the customary middle-class dinner party seating arrangement (Man, Woman, Man, Woman, Closet Homosexual, Rampantly Public Homosexual, Bitter Divorcee, Bitter Divorcee, Feuding Workmate, Feuding Workmate, Recovering Alkie, Recovering Bulimic, Desperate Singleton, Pregnant Person Who Won't Talk About Anything Except Her Pregnancy.)

Whilst your guests make small talk, return to the kitchen.

Your oven should now be sufficiently pre-heated. Place all discarded supermarket packaging and receipts into the oven and incinerate to dispose of incriminating evidence.

Deflect all oncoming compliments about your culinary skill using a coy and modest smile.

How To Be Complimentary When Confronted With An Exceedingly Ugly Baby

He's very... unusual looking...

Try not to panic.
Remember! Nursing mothers can be extremely ferocious when provoked.

Do not shout or scream.
In particular, do not shout 'Uuurgh!' or scream that the baby resembles that thing from *Alien* that burst out of John Hurt's stomach.

With a slow, unhurried motion, turn your head away from the baby.
You may experience feelings of nausea. Try to control the urge to vomit.

Cover your face with your hands. Avoid looking directly at the parents.
Shield your eyes to minimise the risk of accidental revulsion. Close your mouth to prevent dangerously honest remarks.

Assume a captivated smile, placing the corners of the mouth in an upturned position
This move is useful in a variety of social situations and is known by masters as 'Adopting An Entranced Expression Despite Inner Revulsion'.

Retreat several feet.
Try to put as many adoring relatives between yourself and the ugly baby as you can. They will emit complimentary remarks which should absorb the impact of the baby's ugliness.

Deflect any questions about the baby's adorability using a well-timed cough or sneeze.
Cover your disgust with a non-committal reply.

Advise placing the ugly baby in a darkened room.
Wrap any disfigured body parts with a cute T-shirt or romper suit.

If the parents still appear uneasy, take a deep breath and place your lips near to the baby's mouth.
Administer a swift kiss and 'coochie-coo'. Do not administer a series of sharp blows to the chest with the palm of your outstretched hand.

Alert oncoming visitors of the baby's ugliness.
Prior warning may afford them the vital minutes required to don dark glasses or a protective facial mask.

Back away slowly.
When you spot a suitable exit route, make your escape.

It should be safe to return to the child within approximately 18 years.
Such ugliness is normally temporary and should pass by the end of puberty.

If ugliness persists, get the afflicted child to a qualified plastic surgeon as soon as possible.
DO NOT wrap the ugly baby in a blanket and throw it from an upstairs window, except in the most extreme of emergencies.

How To Evade Vegetarian Food

Know your enemy.
Like Terrorism and Sectarianism, Vegetarianism is an increasing threat to civilised Western society. Militant anti-meat-eating factions, such as the notorious Hummous, may attack at random in restaurants and snackbars, often using tofu and TVP (Textured Vegetable Protein) cunningly disguised as normal food.

Stay within a known safe area.
Restrict yourself to regions within the Axis of Offal, such as Aberdeen Steak Houses and branches of Dewhursts Butchers.

If you are unwittingly lured into a vegetarian restaurant, remain calm.
Vegetarians are normally too weak and undernourished to present a physical threat.

Do not antagonise the enemy by revealing yourself to be a Meat Eater.
Try to mimic Vegan tendencies. Emit weedy, feeble-sounding coughs at regular intervals. Visit the toilet and dampen your hair to make it appear lank and greasy. If approached, keep your mouth closed and hum the first Morrissey song you can remember.

When the food arrives, lick your lips and feign an appetite.

Carefully make an incision into the TVP with the knife provided, then puncture it with the fork. Lift the TVP towards the mouth, but DO NOT eat it. Act as though your attention has been distracted just before the moment of morsel consumption, or suddenly think of something interesting to say about Battery Farming.

Look for places to hide your unwanted vegetarian meal.

These could include in a napkin, under a large lettuce leaf, or up your sleeve. Do not attempt to hide any of it in your stomach, unless you have first dismembered the meal and inserted it inside a condom. This will prevent it leaking out into your alimentary canal, and may also render the taste a little less bland and rubbery.

Manoeuvre the pieces of food around the plate until the waiter comes back and takes your dishes away.

If challenged about your lack of appetite, explain that you are on a strict new Fruitarian/Vitamin Pillarian/Oxygenerian diet regime, for religious reasons.

Make your escape, but DO NOT run.

This will also betray your status as a non-Vegetarian. Exit the restaurant by shuffling slowly towards the door, keeping your legs bowed to suggest chronic Vitamin C deficiency and snuffling in a pronounced manner.

HOW TO EVADE VEGETARIAN FOOD

When safely out of view of the restaurant, hail a cab and proceed at maximum velocity to the nearest fast-food joint or kebab shop.

If stranded in an exceptionally backward civilisation with neither a MacDonalds nor a Burger King, resort to cannibalism. Lightly grilled vegetarians make a tasty snack if snapped in half and dipped in warm cheese fondue.

How to Fend Off A Former Partner On *Jerry Springer*

Stay calm.
Make no sudden confessions. This will merely excite the audience and give them a taste for blood.

Fluff up your hair, making it as big as possible. Use backcombing and a toupee if necessary.
This will make you appear more intimidating. It will also make you appear more American, and may elicit sympathy from Mr Springer.

Make a growling or snarling noise.
Such as, 'But what about the time YOU slept with MY handicapped teenage sister? HUH?'

Cry. A lot.
Remember, a ravenous audience will never attack the weakest and most vulnerable member of the group.

Shout for psychiatric help.
Wave your arms in a scary lunatic fashion.

Using a Regression Therapist if necessary, retreat slowly backwards into your childhood.
You should encounter a recollection of parental abuse. If not, use your skill and cunning to make one up. This will

stop an attacking audience member in its tracks and cause it to attack your father instead.

If your father is already dead, you may have to:
a) Weep over the loss of a beloved parent, or
b) Reveal that he wasn't your real dad at all, claim you were adopted, and blame your biological father for ruining your life instead.

Assume the foetal position.
Rock gently from side to side, sobbing uncontrollably.

Call for sympathy.
Mr Springer may become docile and stroke your hair fondly. DO NOT allow Mr Springer to lick you or bite your neck. Mr Springer is a venomous rat-like creature and will attempt to lure you into his lair (or hotel room).

Take cover behind the largest object you can find.
Such as Mr Springer's ego, or a 35-stone fellow studio guest waiting to appear on the 'Alien Abduction Drove Me To Cheat' episode of the programme.

When the adverts arrive, make a run for the studio door.
Do not stop until you are well out of camera-shot.

Dial the emergency services and request prompt Legal Aid.
You should be able to sue Mr Springer for at least $1m.

How To Find The Loo In A Huge Modern Gastro-Dome

This is not a mission to be attempted by the inexperienced! Many weak-bladdered individuals have perished after losing their way and wandering for days in the cavernous depths of London's trendy mega-eateries.

Try to eliminate the need for urination or defecation during your meal. This can be achieved by being seated at the worst table in the restaurant, thus ensuring the waiter rarely, if ever, delivers any food or drink to you.

If you cannot resist the urge to void your bowels, maximise your survival chances by ensuring you follow the procedure below:

Place as much of your meal as possible into the centre of a napkin. Draw together the four corners and knot securely to form a parcel.
Suspend this on a breadstick (or in the event of being in a Chinese restaurant, a chopstick) and sling this over your shoulder. You will need all the sustenance you can get to avoid suffering malnutrition during your journey.

Locate the pepper mill.
In most restaurants, this will be the item resembling a three-foot-tall dildo with a huge bell end.

Sniff the air: try to determine a faint scent of human excrement or urine.

Warning! This can be misleading. If asparagus is on the menu, this scent may be emanating from the kitchen.

Scrutinise the surrounding area – look for fresh stools or spray markings that may have been left by desperate fellow patrons on their way to the Toilets.

Head out in the most promising direction.

As you proceed, leave a trail of pepper behind you.

If your expedition is successful, this will enable you to retrace your steps back to your table.

Keep your blood-sugar level up by scavenging for sugar lumps from unattended tables.

Avoid any 'wraps' of unidentifiable white powder: these may look like pure sugar, but in fact may be cut with Canderel, Sweet n Low or (in restaurants with a large clientele from the media industry) cocaine.

If you get really lost, try making fire to send up a smoke signal.

With luck, a Waiter will appear to tell you that Smoking Is Only Permitted in The Smoking Section, and you can interrogate him as to the whereabouts of the Toilets.

When you reach the Toilets, STOP!
Your mission is still not complete.

In front of you will be two doors, which to the untrained eye may appear identical.
Entering via the wrong door could have potentially fatal consequences!

Even if you are absolutely bursting, take several moments to scrutinise the two doors.
On each door you should be able to make out a strange, tribal hieroglyphic, one of which may look vaguely like a woman and the other, vaguely like a man.

This is a trick designed to cause maximum embarrassment to those unacquainted with the mysterious ways of modern Trendy Restaurants.
If you are a man, enter via the door with the symbol least resembling a human male.

If you are a woman, enter via the door with the symbol least resembling a human female.

If you are a game show host, Take Your Pick.

Having successfully accomplished the passing of a motion, retrace your steps to your table by following the pepper trail.
Adopt a 'Scout's Pace' - alternately running 20 steps, walking 20 steps, and spending 20 seconds slapping away the hand of the homosexual waiter who is inevitably hovering behind you as you exit the lavatory area.

To avoid rickets or malnutrition, ingest small regular meals along the way from your Food Parcel.

Conserve as much energy as you can for a final burst of speed.

Be prepared for a shock. When you reach the table your Bill may have arrived. You and your dining companion will probably need to do a runner.

How To Survive If The Earth Fails To Move (For Women)

To avoid disappointing your lover, you must react as if caught in the epicentre of an earthquake measuring at least 5.8 on the Richter Scale.
Extinguish all lights, naked flames or soft romantic candles. Acting under cover of darkness will minimise the risk of your faked orgasm being discovered.

Lie back, remove any excess clothing and brace yourself for a Crap Shag.
Your lover may be a crap shag without warning, or he may

alert you to his sexual ineptitude by being a lousy kisser, possessing an unfeasibly shiny red car, or responding to queries about his bedroom prowess by chuckling 'Well, hur-hur, I've never had any complaints in THAT department, babe!'

Allow sufficient time for your lover to satisfy himself.

Thirty seconds will normally be adequate. Then initiate the Faking procedure.

Your legs should begin to tremble slightly, with the tremors moving gradually upward towards the knees and crotch region.

It may help to grasp the bedposts tightly for extra support, and perform a series of seemingly involuntary pelvic thrusts.

Open your mouth and scream to alert your lover that you are coming.

It is best not to scream loudly enough to alert the neighbours or the Emergency Services. Nor is it necessary to blow a loud whistle or set off distress flares.

Close the eyes, tense the facial muscles and contort your features into a twisted mask of apparent ecstasy.

Ensure that the curtains are drawn and that you and your lover are well out of public view. Abuse of Ecstasy in this way is still a criminal offence in the United Kingdom.

Between screams, utter an internationally recognised codeword such as 'Oh God!' or 'Yes, Yes, YES!' or 'AAAAAAAAAAAAAARGH!'

You should also shout your lover's name (if known). If unsure about your lover's name, do not shout anything. Uttering the name of a previous lover may enrage him and lead to undue bloodshed.

When satisfied of your lover's mistaken belief that he's satisfied you and transported you to previously unimaginable heights of passion, cease writhing and gasping for breath.

Lie motionless for several seconds in order to feign a contented afterglow.

Refrain from any further moaning.

Even if he was REALLY crap in bed.

Wait for someone to inquire about your physical wellbeing.

Your lover should ask whether it was 'good for you too'. (Though this is not compulsory, and he may not give a monkey's whether it was or not.)

Reply in the affirmative.

Ensure that you keep your fingers crossed. And your legs, lest your Inept Lover think he needs to prove his manhood by giving you another Multiple Orgasm.

CHAPTER SEVEN

Dealing With Dangerous Animals

How To Extract Your Leg From A Randy Dog

He likes you...

A Randy Dog is vastly more dangerous to your dignity than a Rabid Dog.

Learn to identify the telltale signs of randiness before the dog has a chance to assault you.

Has the dog entered the country from abroad? Dogs returning from France may be feeling particularly passionate.

Is the dog licking its lips excessively, or foaming at the penis?

Does it have a prominent stiffy and look as though it would come when you called its name, probably leaving a nasty stain on your turn-ups?

Deter the dog by ensuring that your legs and feet are particularly sexually unattractive.

Wear Green Flash trainers and golfing trousers. Do not tread in any dog poo, which is the canine equivalent of sloshing an entire bottle of Calvin Klein's 'Obsession' down your cleavage.

Try to back off without attracting the Randy Dog's attention.

Move slowly and deliberately. If the dog continues its approach, shout 'NO! DOWN BOY!' Unfortunately this is normally insufficient to deter Randy Dogs (or, for that matter, Randy Human Males).

Kick the dog in the teeth.

Beware! If the dog is a foot fetishist, this may simply increase his ardour.

Using your free leg to propel you sideways in a crab-like motion, try to shuffle towards a table or similar item of heavy furniture.

The table may have more sexually alluring legs than you do, especially if it's one of those hand-carved Queen Anne style ones.

Call the police.

Demand a team of professional Dog Handlers. They may be able to pull the dog off. If they cannot actually pull him off, they might at least be able to fondle him a bit or distract his attention with a sexy Alsatian bitch.

If you cannot detach the dog using brute force, the dog may have to be put down.

Put the dog down by mocking its sexual prowess or telling it you've seen Chihuahuas with bigger willies.

The dog should back off immediately to lick its wounded pride.

Or its own bollocks. Men should try to contain their feelings of jealousy at this point.

How To Avoid A Bite From An Angry Hamster

The Golden Hamster *(Mesocricetus auratus)* is not indigenous to the UK, but may be encountered in such areas as children's bedrooms, school classrooms and pet shops.

The natural habitat of this rodent is a translucent space-station with interconnecting tubes, a plastic treadmill and a 'penthouse apartment' the size of a studio flat in Earl's Court.

Caution! Incidence of Hamster bites is especially high around the Christmas period, when Hamsters may be lurking inside brightly-wrapped presents waiting to ambush unsuspecting Mums and Dads. Always wear gloves when opening suspicious Christmas packages. If in doubt, shake the package vigorously to see if it squeaks.

Do not attempt to pick up the Hamster immediately.
Hamsters are your enemy. They can smell your fear.

To render the Hamster's bite harmless, go to the bathroom cabinet and equip yourself with suitable supplies.
Waterproof Elastoplast, antiseptic cream and a cotton wool swab are unnecessary. You will need: I box of tampons

(Super or Super Plus absorbency, depending on the size and weight of the Hamster).

Remove one tampon from its packaging and extend the blue string to its full length.

Holding the tampon by the string, poke it through the bars of the hamster cage. The Hamster will be fooled into thinking this is your finger, and will sink its jaws into the tampon.

Wait until the Hamster has inserted the entire tampon into its cheek pouch.

Repeat the process with a second tampon, which should be inserted into the opposite pouch.

Now ensure that the Hamster has access to a liberal supply of fresh water.

As soon as the Hamster drinks the water, its cheek pouches will swell up to ten times their previous size, thus immobilising the beast's jaws.

Open the cage door and pick up the Hamster using the two blue strings dangling from its mouth.

Handling of the Hamster is now a simple and risk-free process. Hamsters which have been exhausted of their entertainment value or superseded by the latest Pokémon toy may be usefully recycled as charming festive decorations simply by attaching them by the blue string to the branches of your Christmas tree.

To dispose of unwanted Hamsters on Boxing Day, light the blue string with a match and retire to a safe distance.

Barbecued Hamster chunks can be freeze-dried and kept for up to six months in a backpack to provide emergency nourishment on hiking expeditions or when lost in the mountains. They are high in protein and have a piquant, chicken-like taste, which is considered a delicacy in many foreign countries.

How To Survive An Alien Abduction

Minimise the chance of Alien Attack by wearing suitable repellent clothing, such as a hat made of folded aluminium foil.

Or a particularly unflattering shellsuit. This will also minimise the likelihood of your being sexually experimented on by other human beings of the opposite gender.

If you find yourself confronted by Aliens, do not panic.
It could be worse. They could be Millwall fans, or timeshare salesmen.

Assess the situation rationally.
Is the life form in front of you roughly humanoid in shape, but only 60 per cent of the size of a normal adult? Does it have greyish, papery, slightly crenellated skin? Is its head large and bony with huge, deep-set staring eyes and pinched features, and its body small and skinny with a distended midriff and neither breasts nor male genitalia? Does it appear to be naked, or wearing nothing which is immediately recognisable as human clothing? If so, there is no need to panic. You have simply come face-to-face with Geri Halliwell. Back off slowly, to avoid her attempting to take you hostage and subject you to bizarre and involuntary sexual experimentation.

If the life forms are definitely alien to Planet Earth, reassure them that you are not hostile by transmitting universal Friendship Messages.
Such as 'Wotcher mate!', 'Pukkaaaah!' and 'Y'alright then, our kid?'

Comply fully with the Aliens' request for you to take them to your Leader.
Direct the Aliens to Number Ten, Downing Street. Here you can rest assured that they will be rapidly detained, incarcerated without trial and deported on the next Eurostar Express under suspicion of being Illegal Immigrants. Any immediate threat to British civilisation will thus be successfully neutralised.

The Little Book of Books

by Debbie Barham

If you don't know your Harry Potter from your Harold Pinter, then this is the only publication you'll ever need! Too stressed to read *The Little Book of Calm*? No time to plough through *A Brief History of Time*? Too depressed to open *Prozac Nation*? This Little Book of Literature is a complete library in your pocket.

The Little Book of Weddings

by Debbie Barham

If tying the knot has your stomach knotting up with Pre-Marital Tension, don't panic! With jokes old, new, borrowed and blue, this Little Book of Big Days will put a smile on the face of any Happy Couple. Stuffed with more pages than a promiscuous bridesmaid, it unveils all the 'I Do's' and Don'ts of getting hitched without a hitch.

www.summersdale.com